Never Take **NO** for an Answer

Dear Sue —
Wishing you abundance
and wealth.
Karen Sheridan

Never Take NO for an Answer

One Woman, One Life,
and
The Money Mystique

Karen Sheridan

BookPartners, Inc.
Wilsonville, Oregon

BookPartners, Inc.
P.O. Box 922
Wilsonville, Oregon 97070

DEDICATION

To Mother, for teaching me about love.

To Dad, for teaching me about life.

To my brother and sisters, for teaching me about laughter.

To Lisa and Mark, for teaching me about light.

To friends, for teaching me about loyalty.

And to those who taught me about the Money Mystique.

– Karen Sheridan

ACKNOWLEDGEMENTS

This book is dedicated to the many people who encouraged me to speak in my own voice. It was a long time coming. Timing is everything, and these people came into my life at the right time. Each of you has given me the opportunity to learn more about myself, without judgment.

Patti Adams	Pamela Jones	Vivian Stapley
Joyce Allmon	Carolyn Laughlin	Gloria Strait
Anne Bunick	Cindi McFarland	Sheila Titus
Nick Bunick	Carol Moore	Karen Torrell
Elaine Burroughs	Jacques Nichols	Billye Turner
Paul Halliday	Pete and Kit Ryan	Diane West
Mrs. Jackson	Steve Sheridan	

I am grateful for my wonderful children, Lisa and Mark, who taught me about love, commitment and personal growth. No mother loves or respects her children more.

I would be remiss in not acknowledging Ursula and Thorn Bacon of BookPartners who encouraged me to use my life as a way to teach money stories rather than to write just another book about money management. Without them, this book would not exist.

I also celebrate the wonderful women who have already put aside their money fears and come to my workshop anyway. Thank you for taking care of yourselves and supporting The Money Mystique.

It scares me to put this in writing because I know I have probably missed someone who should be named on this page. If this is you, please accept my deepest gratitude and my heartfelt apologies. It doesn't diminish your contribution to my life in any way.

Thank you all for enriching my life in your own unique way.

One last word:

This book contains material based upon my personal recollection of events as they happened in my life. No doubt some people who were involved could tell a different story. I have no intention of embarrassing or hurting anybody. I do, however, believe in telling the truth — as I experienced it — through my own filters. To quote Shelley, "Where is the love, beauty and truth we seek, but in our mind?"

CHAPTER ONE

~ ~ ~ ~ ~ ~ ~ ~ ~ ~ ~ ~ ~ ~ ~ ~ ~ ~ ~

"It's a funny thing about life; if you refuse to accept anything but the best, you very often get it."

— Somerset Maugham

Dear Mother,

It's been so long since we talked. I want to call you, but I don't know how. So, I am writing you this letter knowing you are still my greatest fan. I wish you had been here the past seven years because so much has happened.

I finally graduated from college — thirty-one years after I started. And they said I wouldn't finish! Unfortunately, I was sick as a dog on graduation day and couldn't go to the ceremony. But I know I have the degree and that's all that matters. I've

~ ~ ~ ~ ~ ~ ~ ~ ~ ~ ~ ~ ~ ~ ~ ~ ~ ~ ~ ~

decided to get a doctorate by the time I'm seventy. Gives me something to work toward.

I got tired of banging my head against the glass ceiling and left the corporate world for good when I was rather unceremoniously bounced out of my last big job. I went from vice president to unemployed in one fell swoop. Guess I could have gotten back in the race, but it's too much work as a woman just to get along — forget doing the job.

The timing was rather dramatic because I filed for divorce from Steve and sold my house that same week. The Universe really helped me understand big changes were needed and provided them. It took me no time at all to adjust. I was ready to live in harmony with myself and my surroundings. Not a day goes by that I don't thank God for putting me where I am right now.

You would absolutely love my house. It's smaller than my others, but it is cozy and it's mine. There isn't a thing in it that doesn't mean something to me. Like the old pictures of your sisters who died so young, the plate Grandma and Grandpa received at their wedding, and the porcelain figurines you and Dad got for your wedding. Lots of things from our trip around the world and gifts from friends. It's a wonderful place to be. Everything is beautiful. Sometimes I feel like Martha Stewart. I spend more time as a human being than as a human doing, so it's nice to have a place to be. I feel safe.

I live with two darling cats, Murphy and Morgan. They are Scottish folds with darling folded ears. Who ever would have believed I'd be a cat lover? Guess that says tons about enjoying life rather than making it so difficult. I used to believe I

~ ~ ~ ~ ~ ~ ~ ~ ~ ~ ~ ~ ~ ~ ~ ~ ~ ~ ~

had to work hard for everything. Now I realize abundance is everywhere, and it comes into my life rather effortlessly.

And my garden! You wouldn't believe the garden. Flowers, flowers everywhere. It's all put to bed now, but come spring it will be reborn again. I've learned the botanical names of my flowers and can see the garden from every room in the house. It is my greatest source of self-expression. I love how it changes month to month spring through fall. You would enjoy it.

It took courage to end my marriage to Steve. Guess it was time for Karen to take care of Karen — but it was hard. I loved him so much, but I just wasn't happy in the marriage. Too much conflict. I wish it had turned out differently, but it didn't.

One thing Steve said was that I couldn't teach women about money because I am "Too stupid in math." I may not be very good at math, but I am good at teaching women about money.

And that is what I want to tell you. I support myself by teaching women about money. It was always a mystery to me how I could go from being a housewife in Oregon to being a vice president on Wall Street in just six years. I am still not sure how I did it, but I do know why I did it.

I've always believed there is a great purpose to life (I call it my "soul purpose"), and it was my responsibility to find it — and then act on it. Losing my husband, my house and my job simultaneously gave me time to examine my life and my talents — to explore my dreams. It forced me to sit back, relax, and take a deep breath. When I opened my eyes, it was clear to me I had to work with women and their money. Every life experience I had

~ ~ ~ ~ ~ ~ ~ ~ ~ ~ ~ ~ ~ ~ ~ ~ ~ ~ ~

pointed me in this direction. Scary as it was, I started with my first workshop in July of 1994. I can hardly believe it happened so fast.

Cindi, my manicurist, got seven women to come to the first workshop. I had three weeks to put a program together. As usual, being a "just-in-time" kind of person, I didn't have a clue as to what I was going to do. So I rented a house at the beach, took all my books and news articles along, and wrote the first part of the four-part series. I worked day and night for three weeks and finished the day before the first meeting. It was a success.

The women wanted to meet again in two weeks. Omigod! Now what was I to do? The obvious topics were taxes, estate planning and insurance. The problem was, I didn't know beans about any of these topics. Creativity came to my rescue and I put together a pretty good presentation. For instance, I didn't talk about standard deductions and adjusted gross income. I talked about the history of the federal tax system and put it in the context of what is happening in Washington today — creating a basis for understanding.

Then they wanted to come back in another two weeks to learn about the stock market and mutual funds. For the last session I prepared information about the bond market and how to put a portfolio together.

The whole thing damn near killed me. I worked day and night for two months. I spent hours in the library trying to get a handle on the psychology of money and why people are so afraid of it. I've tried to understand how to help women use money to express themselves and to enjoy their lives. I wrote a glossary for every subject in

~ ~

everyday language. I sat at the computer until midnight night after night. But, you know, mother, it was all in me, just yearning to come out.

This fall I started working with women in support groups. I call this series Masterminding Your Money. This is a safe place for women to explore their dreams and life purpose, and miracles happen! The goal is to create the money to live your life dream. When I get scared I won't have the money to make my house payment or to buy something for the business, I know I have to trust and take the plunge. Again and again it turns out to be the right thing. I can't even explain how it works; it just does. And, it works for my clients too. I see it every day. These women who come to my workshops go away empowered in a way they didn't believe possible.

What is it about money that makes women so hesitant to invest it? Why don't they enjoy their money? Because they think of money in terms of whether or not they have enough and they are afraid. I believe we need to understand how we want to express ourselves, and then create the money to express ourselves in that way. It turns the idea of money upside down, and it works. I do it in my own life every day.

You know, Mother, my life really makes sense for the first time. It's easy. I live without fear. I don't have big decisions about what to do because I know what to do. It takes no willpower or force of will. The hardest part is making myself stop to rest. I am so happy.

I can't tell you how much I miss you. Even though you are not here in the physical world, you are always with me. So much of me is you. I can still

~ ~

hear your laugh and see your beautiful brown eyes
sparkle. Thanks for believing in me.
   'Til we meet again.
      Love,
       Karen
       xoxoxo

CHAPTER TWO

~ ~ ~ ~ ~ ~ ~ ~ ~ ~ ~ ~ ~ ~ ~ ~ ~ ~ ~

"Life is either a daring adventure or it is nothing."
– Helen Keller

As I look back on the adventure that has been my life, I realize I have certainly had my share of ups and downs. A friend of mine once told me, "You have the best of everything and the worst of everything. You can go from my prayer list to my hit list in less than twenty-four hours."

It may sound strange, and perhaps even vague or irrational to say I always believed I was born for something bigger than myself. But that's the way I felt. One day, I wanted to be able to look back on my life and feel I had accomplished something important; I just didn't have a clue what it would be. One thing was for sure: I wanted my life to be an adventure.

~ ~ ~ ~ ~ ~ ~ ~ ~ ~ ~ ~ ~ ~ ~ ~ ~ ~ ~

As I retrace the steps that led me to where I am today, I come face to face with my life and my accomplishments. How did I turn a self-absorbed and fearful woman into a person who is living her life purpose? How did it happen? I am a woman who doesn't doubt herself. I never limited myself and, consequently, I've never taken "No" for an answer. Oh, I've thrown in the towel a time or two, but basically, if I set my sights on something, I pursue it with the same tenacity as that last leaf clinging to the tree in the depth of winter.

I have a passion for life itself and nearly everything I do. I always invest all of me in the job at hand, whether it is raising children, knitting a sweater, or marketing the services of a giant Wall Street investment firm.

I have waltzed into places totally new to me looking for opportunities. I interviewed the interviewer, carefully listening to the messages and nuances behind the words. Consequently, I staked my claim and for some reason unknown even to me, I never doubted my willingness and ability to do the job — whatever the job. I never entertained the thought I couldn't do something. Even though I rarely knew how to do it — I always knew I would accomplish what I set out to do.

The theme of my story is contained in a statement Eleanor Roosevelt made: "If you say you can, you can. If you say you can't, you can't."

It's really pretty simple.

Call me brash and stubborn. Call me full of myself. But I guess I've always liked the idea of plunging over the edge, somehow knowing I will land on my feet. F. Scott Fitzgerald's words apply to me when he wrote: "Draw your chair close to the edge of the precipice, and I will tell you a story."

~ ~ ~ ~ ~ ~ ~ ~ ~ ~ ~ ~ ~ ~ ~ ~ ~ ~ ~ ~

It's my story, and I hope that you will find a message in it for yourself that just may bring a fresh view, a new understanding of the complexities of your own life experiences.

The roots of my strict and traditional Utah upbringing were deeply imbedded in my family's religious beliefs, which promised me no more than a happy married life and children. Where I come from, women are looked upon as second-rate citizens, somehow less than men. Marriage and raising lots of children was the womanly thing to do — and that was all right. I wanted to get married and have children and be happy. But I also wanted more, even though I didn't know what "more" meant.

Like other women, there always has been — and always will be in me — an undeniable determination coupled with an insatiable curiosity to learn, to know and to use my talents to their fullest potential. There were moments when I was actually afraid, sensing how powerful I really was. As Marianne Williamson said, "Our deepest fear is that we are powerful beyond measure."

Yet, there I was in a traditionally patriarchal culture that laid out my future for me — limited at best. I knew that wasn't right. Only I didn't know what to do about it the first fifty years of my life. It is only through conscious living and listening to that persistent inner voice of rebellion that I have learned to express myself without shame. It feels wonderful!

Some friends and members of my family have described me as complicated, prickly, hardheaded, and perhaps overconfident. And, considering the various

~ ~ ~ ~ ~ ~ ~ ~ ~ ~ ~ ~ ~ ~ ~ ~ ~ ~ ~

circumstances in which I found myself here and there, I am sure these observations often applied.

I didn't know how or where or when, but I knew I would have to find self-expression in a different way — in a way that was unacceptable to my family's beliefs and tradition. All this left me feeling sad and alone. I so wanted to believe and react the way my friends did, but I just couldn't. With an indescribable yearning, something inside of me was pulling me away from "what was expected of me." I wanted to do things differently — *my* agenda — and that wasn't possible in the environment where I grew up.

Most of my friends didn't go to college. As girls, we were literally told that all we had to do was to grow up and get married, and that didn't require an education. I went off to the University of Utah on a scholarship in 1959, fully believing I could conquer the world, like most high school graduates. The world was waiting for me, and I was ready. College promised to be fun as well.

As it turned out, there wasn't much time for fun. All through college, I had to work — and work hard. I assisted the bookkeeper of a wholesale produce company. Six days a week, I reported to work at four o'clock in the morning. This meant getting up before the crack of dawn and hitting the road. I didn't mind it so much, because the men I worked with taught me a lot about life I didn't learn at home. It was quite an eye-opener. I remember a foreman coming in one morning, telling me to close my eyes and open my hand. I dutifully complied, only to feel something cold and furry crawling through my fingers. I nearly fainted when I realized it was a huge tarantula spider he had discovered dormant in the bananas. I screamed and everybody laughed. I still think of Joe and the tarantula when I see a bunch of bananas. I'm always good for a laugh.

~ ~ ~ ~ ~ ~ ~ ~ ~ ~ ~ ~ ~ ~ ~ ~ ~ ~ ~ ~

Between working hard, attending classes and studying, there was little room left for fun and friends, not to mention dating. But I wanted that degree more than anything and was willing to put up with the hardships of having to earn the money to pay for it.

Finally, with just two quarters left to go, I had saved enough money to quit my job. I would be able to finish school without having to work, provided I could live rent-free at home. I approached my father asking him if I could quit my job and move back home for those two quarters. My father was a hard man, but my request was so reasonable that I could not imagine his refusing me.

His curt, cold "No" was like a blow.

I'll never forget my lost feeling, the painful wave of disappointment and disillusionment struck me like cold water in my face. I knew that pleading with him was useless. For him to change his mind was a sign of weakness. I was plain tired and worn out from my crazy schedule. My parents weren't getting along very well at the time, and things were uncomfortable at home. I realized I had more than outgrown home anyway — it was time to move on.

The next problem I had to solve was where to go? What I really wanted to do was go around the world. But I didn't have the confidence or the money for that. So I decided to make Portland, Oregon, my first stop. A good friend of mine was raised in Portland and told me what a nice city it was. Then there was my friend Lyn, who was at loose ends as well and ready to spread her wings. She decided to come along with me to explore the Northwest.

I quit my job and packed my bags.

Ticket in hand, luggage checked, I waited to board my flight while I said a teary goodbye to my parents, who came along to see me off. I kept looking around for signs of Lyn;

~ ~ ~ ~ ~ ~ ~ ~ ~ ~ ~ ~ ~ ~ ~ ~ ~ ~ ~ ~

after all she represented part of home and familiarity for me, and a sort of stability which my mother heartily endorsed.

Lyn stood me up. Later I found out that she and her boyfriend had run off and gotten married! A fine time to let me know. I could see a blink of hope-eternal in my mother's eyes for a brief moment when Lyn failed to arrive. She was sure I wouldn't dare go off alone.

She looked at me and said, "I guess you won't be going." But I shook my head and said, "I guess I'll go alone." Nothing, no one could have stopped me. Mother and Dad would have to return home without me. I was on my way. Freedom, here I come!

Blessings do come in the darndest disguises, and in retrospect I think it was just as well that my friend reneged. Perhaps we would have returned home if we found ourselves broke and lonely in a strange city by building on each other's fears and worries.

I landed in Portland with $300 in my pocket, a head full of dreams, unbridled energy and scared to death. Thoughts bounced through my head like ping pong balls. I kept thinking, what am I doing here? How will I support myself? I don't even have a college degree! I don't know anybody here. This is just a hare-brained scheme I've hatched. How am I going to get myself out of this? Will I be embarrassed to go back to Utah with my tail between my legs?

At the same time, my negative mind chatter was trying to undermine my confidence, my high-in-the-sky expecta-tions buoyed me up, making me tingle with excitement. On the one hand, I thought I couldn't make it on my own; on the other hand, I was determined to build a life for myself away from the influence of the Mormon Church. Being a Mormon worked for lots of people, but not for me. I wanted

~ ~ ~ ~ ~ ~ ~ ~ ~ ~ ~ ~ ~ ~ ~ ~ ~ ~ ~ ~

to be in a place where I could be my own person. I felt free for the first time in my life. Nobody had any expectations of me — I answered to no one. I could stop pretending. I could be whoever I wanted to be. It was a new beginning in more ways than one.

Portland was beautiful — clean and green, small enough to be sane, big enough to be interesting. Sure, it wasn't New York City, but people were as friendly as the flowers they grew. Portland seemed as good a place as any for my adventure to begin. School would have to wait; life wouldn't.

When things got a little tight, I was able to move in with the mother of a college friend, who gave me a few lessons in living I've never forgotten. Philis was fifty, which seemed old to me at the time, but she was certainly young at heart. She read everything she could lay her hands on, loved life and spent weekends at a nudist colony. I had never met anyone like her. She certainly didn't fit in with the women whom I had grown up with. My role models were more like the Stepford Wives.

But by the end of three weeks, I was feeling pretty lonely. It was the Fourth of July weekend. Philis was out of town, I was around people I didn't really know, and I missed my family. If I was ever tempted to throw in the towel and go home, it was that weekend. But a reassuring voice in me kept saying, "You can do it. You can make a life for yourself — a life that makes sense."

I stuck it out.

After a few weeks, I found a job as secretary in the personnel department of Goodwill Industries. I had interviewed with several companies, but when I landed at Goodwill, I knew it was the place for me. I had never been around people with disabilities, and I wanted to do my part

~ ~ ~ ~ ~ ~ ~ ~ ~ ~ ~ ~ ~ ~ ~ ~ ~ ~ ~ ~

to help them achieve their potential.

I loved my work, and within a few months I was promoted to employment counselor. It was a challenging job and offered me an opportunity to really make a difference in people's lives. It felt good to help the less fortunate find work. The rest would be up to them. One manager referred to me as "a ray of sunshine with a rod of steel up her back." I wasn't quite sure what she meant, but I took it as a compliment.

I met Gary just three months into my new life. Tall and slender, with blond hair, he had a gentle face with an easy smile. He appeared so much older and self-assured at twenty-five than I felt at the age of twenty-one. I knew he was my Prince Charming, and an altogether nice man. He became my anchor — and I needed one.

I had so many unresolved issues stemming from my childhood, and I went off the charts with my exhilarating highs and bottoming-out lows. When my emotions soared to dizzy heights or dropped to gloomy lows, when my life didn't move the way I wanted and I was all over the place, Gary was still and calm, centered and reassuring — so different from me. He was the kind of person who said "No" to cake because he wasn't hungry. I, on the other hand, didn't think hunger had anything to do with eating cake. But that was Gary — no addictions, no passions, no nonsense — solid.

Gary and I were married in 1963, nine months after we met and one year after I moved to Portland. I was barely twenty-two years old and Gary was nearly a ripe old twenty-six. We were joined at the hip from our very first meeting, and that lasted for twenty years.

I placed my feet firmly on the path of marriage and home, complete with picket fence, and children — the path

~ ~ ~ ~ ~ ~ ~ ~ ~ ~ ~ ~ ~ ~ ~ ~ ~ ~ ~ ~

that had been carved by Eve and walked by uncountable millions of women before me. I stayed home and took care of the house. I don't believe I was disappointed with myself for choosing home life. I enjoyed being taken care of. Our lifestyle and finances were Gary's job. All I had to do was keep the house in order, prepare the meals, and take care of the children. I had it made.

Eighteen months later, after a difficult pregnancy, our daughter Lisa was born. She was a worry from the start. First of all, she was a breech birth, which had been as hard on her as it was on me. Conscious of what was going on in the delivery room, I heard my doctor say, "Not one baby in a thousand born like this would survive." I burst into tears; I thought my baby had died.

Lisa lived, but she was certainly the worse for the wear. The next day a nurse finally handed me my daughter, and she instructed me to keep the baby wrapped up. At first I abided by her request, but after a while I couldn't stand it any longer. I wanted to see my baby.

I carefully peeled away the thin flannel blanket and unwrapped my little six-pound wonder. Chills still run up and down my spine when I think how tiny and fragile she was as I looked at her for the first time. She had strawberry-blonde curls and a soft down on her face and arms. Her little legs were folded tightly against her doll-like chest, her buns seemed the size of almonds, and she was black from her waist down to her knees. Her small body had taken a merciless beating on its way into this world.

Her neck muscles were pulled out of line; her head was hanging to one side. Her tiny face was swollen like a balloon. She didn't look at all like any of my friends' babies.

Life's challenges for Lisa (as well as for me) had just begun. When she was three weeks old, her doctor told me

~ ~ ~ ~ ~ ~ ~ ~ ~ ~ ~ ~ ~ ~ ~ ~ ~ ~ ~ ~

that she didn't have a hip socket for her right leg, and she would have to spend the next twelve months imprisoned in a hip splint. I couldn't believe my ears. However, the doctor told me that the socket would form eventually, and Lisa would be able to walk normally. Twelve months was a long time away, and at that point just changing her diaper was a major undertaking for me and a painful event for Lisa. Her legs had to be stretched straight out from her sides with the splint placed between them to maintain the position. Without this painful procedure she would grow up with a permanently dislocated hip joint.

Oh, but how it must have hurt. She cried and cried and cried. And, I cried, and cried and cried. Her pitiful wails of protest filled the house night and day. She didn't stop crying for three weeks. How could this wonderful little thing be in so much pain? The phenobarbital the doctor prescribed for her didn't phase her, so I took it to calm me.

Frequently, just to get a way from her screaming, I took walks around the block, cherishing the quiet streets where the only sounds were the chirping of birds and the occasional hum of a lawn mower. Would my baby ever stop crying? Strength, courage and patience had become just words that had lost their meaning and were tired guideposts to bear up under the stress and strain of daily anguish.

About twelve months later, when the cast was finally removed, Lisa was able to walk on her own. Like anything else, pain passes, and relief washed over me with healing grace as I watched my little girl stand on her own two feet. But that wasn't the end of the hardship for her. That little girl had more problems than she bargained for.

As I watched her move about the house, exploring her world, I became aware of the fact that she couldn't see very well. When I read to her, she pushed her nose so close to the

~ ~ ~ ~ ~ ~ ~ ~ ~ ~ ~ ~ ~ ~ ~ ~ ~ ~ ~ ~

pictures that I had to lower the book as I turned the pages. When I told Lisa her grandmother was coming for a visit, she asked me, "What color is she?" I mentioned to my pediatrician that I was worried about my child's vision. He assuaged my concerns by saying, "all first-time mothers worry about their babies." Comfortable advice!

Several months later, I had to face the truth and took Lisa to an ophthalmologist. After checking Lisa's eyes, he turned to me and said, "Your daughter must be an exceptionally bright child. Most people who are that blind couldn't get out of bed in the morning."

The diagnosis was congenital myopia, a condition that would follow her into adulthood. We were told she would always have poor vision. By the time she was twenty-five years old she would be unable to drive a car or even read a newspaper. Not a pretty future. But, we made it through before; we'd make it again.

It was devastating to put thick, bottle-bottom glasses on my beautiful child. There they sat, precariously, on her tiny nose, obscuring her beautiful eyes with their thick double fringe of heavy lashes.

Two-year-old Lisa fought her glasses with the same determination a puppy rejects a leash. I put her glasses on, she tore them off. On, off. On, off. Until one day, as she toddled along, anticipating a step down from one room to another, she sat down and felt for the step with her hand until she felt the edge of it. It was at that moment she must have realized that glasses meant sight and safety. From then on she kept the sight-giving spectacles perched on her little face. Fortunately her vision did not deteriorate any further as she grew, and the adult Lisa, fitted with contact lenses, leads a normal life.

~ ~ ~ ~ ~ ~ ~ ~ ~ ~ ~ ~ ~ ~ ~ ~ ~ ~ ~ ~

I didn't realize then how hard a time she would have growing up. Difficult and heartbreaking as it may have been at times, even for long periods, I wouldn't have traded any of it. Lisa was my greatest teacher.

Mark, on the other hand, who was born when Lisa was two-and-a-half years old, almost raised himself. Our son, with his reddish-brown hair, blue eyes and a sunny disposition, was an easy baby, which was a blessing. Lisa needed a lot more of me. I was fearful at first that something would be wrong with him, and was grateful when there were no problems. Mark was born with a smile on his face and a keen sense of himself. From the very beginning he was self-assured and confident. He was independent and flexible.

To this day, things are easy for Mark. It is strange how two children from the same parents, raised in the same environment, can be so very different. As hard as life has been for Lisa, so has it been easy for her brother. Yet, Lisa has shown us the way to the light.

I believe that raising children is not a hobby, but a full-time job, and I threw myself into the job at hand with a boundless outpouring of energy and a deep sense of purpose. For me it was a labor of love, mixed with an overwhelming feeling of responsibility. Our days were full with visits to the park, the zoo, the science museum and other special places. We saw plays, watched movies, went on picnics and walks, and played together. We had a great time.

There wasn't a craft I didn't pursue. I painted and stitched and knitted and embroidered. I sewed my clothes and Lisa's. I decorated the house from top to bottom even though we didn't have much money. I taught tole-painting lessons so I could buy extra things for the children and the house. And, I read every free minute. Reading let me escape into those other worlds I longed to experience. I dared to

~ ~ ~ ~ ~ ~ ~ ~ ~ ~ ~ ~ ~ ~ ~ ~ ~ ~ ~ ~

dream my own dreams. Dreams are reminders of what we truly want from life. I was confident that I would make my dreams come true.

In the meantime, I stayed close to home, children and hobbies. I remember one Christmas, when I painted hundreds of wooden tree ornaments and dozens of Christmas items and decorations to be sold at a garage sale. I thought it would be nice to turn my hobby into a money-making business. I painted and painted. You couldn't put your foot down anywhere for fear of stepping on a piece of priceless art. There wasn't an inch of space left in my house. I put an ad in the paper, I sent out flyers advertising the big event, and waited for the money to roll in.

The day of the sale finally arrived. I was ready. I waited and waited — the whole weekend long. Not one soul showed up. My husband with his quiet brand of humor, in an attempt to make me laugh, chuckled and said, "It wasn't a total loss, Karen! Two cars slowed down as they drove by."

Sometimes I'd get tired of talking to a bib all day, so when Lisa was out of her cast, I decided to get a part-time job just to have another outlet. I interviewed with Tektronix and was quickly hired for the company's secretarial pool three mornings a week. I lasted one week. Lisa was so unhappy in daycare, I couldn't bear to leave her. So I quit.

But the need to do something more persisted. I considered going back to school part time and finish that degree. I applied and was accepted at Portland State College. When I discussed my plans with Gary, he remained non-committal, and at the time I didn't pursue the matter. When the day came to register for classes, my husband refused to give me the money for tuition. He said, "I didn't think you were really serious. You aren't going anywhere. You've made your bed; now lie in it." I was shocked. Hot anger, resent-

~ ~ ~ ~ ~ ~ ~ ~ ~ ~ ~ ~ ~ ~ ~ ~ ~ ~ ~

ment and disappointment engulfed me like a brush fire.

Gary was my best friend for life, my soul mate — or so I had thought. What had happened? I finally realized that although he was the nicest person in the world, he never talked about himself. Here I thought I had created an environment where he would feel safe to share his feelings.

One day I told him, "I wish I knew you better."

To my amazement he replied, "I can't let you in. I'm afraid you'll hurt me."

I was stunned and came to the conclusion that my marriage was not about sharing feelings; it was about sharing a house. Could I be right? Was our partnership no deeper than the superficial relationship of living together for sexual and protective convenience, two humans sharing space but not ideals and dreams?

I really wanted to believe the way everyone around me did, but I couldn't. I had grown up thinking I was wrong. I had always questioned my ideas and the way I looked at the world. Were my ideas of sharing yet staying independent so idealistic, so inappropriate to reality, that even my husband, my best friend, found them unacceptable? I had always believed I could have my marriage and have myself too. Now I had to face the bitter truth. When my emotions were spent, when my anger and disappointment had played out I felt empty and sad. What would I do about going back to school?

Nothing, I decided. I didn't go back to school for twenty-three years.

I made a truce with myself. If I couldn't be out in the world, I'd make the best of it at home. I watched the children grow and change and grow some more — I was there every step of the way. I did volunteer work, threw myself into home projects and forged close friendships with

~ ~ ~ ~ ~ ~ ~ ~ ~ ~ ~ ~ ~ ~ ~ ~ ~ ~ ~ ~

other women. I decorated our home and gave dinner parties. I pretended everything was wonderful, and tried not to think about what was missing in my life. It is easy to ignore the things you don't acknowledge.

I was too busy watching *That Girl* and *Bewitched* to think about "Life Purpose." I was jarred occasionally when women like Pepper Schwartz, author of the landmark research study *American Couples,* struck a buried note in me when she talked about a woman having "personhood." It hit me like a ton of bricks. What a concept! That meant I wasn't just an appendage to Gary! I could do more than live solely for others and pretend to be fulfilled. It was quite a revelation, and it was disturbing.

While life played itself out within the framework of my family and within the periphery of the proverbial picket fence, other activists like Gloria Steinem and Betty Friedan were making noises about women's roles and the changes we were about to see. These two had the audacity to suggest women had more to contribute than keeping the house clean. Steinem talked about women taking charge of their lives, of becoming doctors, lawyers, CEOs, even president of the United States. I listened with my ears blocked because these high-flying ideas threatened my already shaky ground.

The women's movement and the Vietnam war passed me by. Free love sounded like fun, but I wasn't interested. Life was comfortable. Marriage to Gary — disregarding the deeper differences — was comfortable. He had become quite successful in the real estate business, and we had pretty much everything we wanted.

I enjoyed a special and close relationship with my sister Anne and could count on a circle of wonderful friends for companionship. Family and friends, home and hearth

~ ~ ~ ~ ~ ~ ~ ~ ~ ~ ~ ~ ~ ~ ~ ~ ~ ~ ~ ~

were the golden threads that made the tapestry of my life colorful and pleasant.

That's how it was until one day I was blowing out thirty candles on my birthday cake, and promptly went into a deep slump. How ever did I get to be thirty years old without having the life experiences I longed for as a girl? What had I contributed to the planet? Where had I made a difference? What about my trip around the world? Was this it?

I was devastated but kept my disappointment to myself. Gary remained unaware of the turmoil that boiled within my soul and went cheerfully about his business. We acquired new homes, and each one was bigger and lovelier than the last. I was really quite happy — in an unhappy sort of way. I was busy. Yet, in the midst of this busy-making, sudden waves of unexplained anger would wash over me for no apparent reason. I wondered where it came from. Unable to stop this inner turmoil, I became frightened and confused.

Moodily, I stuffed my panicky depression by telling myself everything was great. At age thirty-two I was living the American dream: a beautiful house full of beautiful things, two new cars in the attached garage, two beautiful and by now healthy children. What more could I possibly want? Just like that kid I'd been in Utah, I didn't dare talk about my feelings because I knew there was something basically wrong with me — so I kept pretending.

I've learned that if we can't make things happen to bring about change, life has a way of doing it for us. I had an accident.

I painted my house from top to bottom, another way to stay busy, and I was in a hurry to finish the front door before I went to my first tennis lesson. Apparently, I didn't

~ ~ ~ ~ ~ ~ ~ ~ ~ ~ ~ ~ ~ ~ ~ ~ ~ ~ ~ ~

position the chair I was using to elongate myself firmly enough. The chair teetered off the porch with me on it — my body went one way and my left leg went the other as I crashed into the bushes. I felt a gut-wrenching pain and saw with horror that the bone in my lower leg was pulled out of joint threatening to come through the skin.

One look was enough to convince me that I was terribly hurt. Years later, a doctor explained the injury to me when he said, "You did the same thing to your leg that you do to a chicken leg when you pull it apart. That's what you did to your knee." The accident destroyed cartilage and ligaments in the knee joint.

Yet the emergency room doctor in the hospital where I sought treatment gave me some aspirin and suggested I see a physician in a few days if I still hurt. One member of the team commented that I couldn't possibly have hurt myself by falling off a chair. I believed him in spite of the excruciating, bone-crushing pain.

The doctor suggested I return if I did not improve. What they didn't recognize was the fact that the short fall off the chair caused as much or more damage to my leg than I might have incurred by playing quarterback for the Dallas Cowboys.

I know it sounds utterly foolish, but we had made plans to go camping with the children and a group of friends that weekend and intended to meet my mother and my step-father in Southern Oregon for a little vacation the following week.

Typical me — even though I was black and blue from the fall and I couldn't straighten my leg; it hurt so badly I couldn't move without experiencing a searing surge of pain — I didn't want to disappoint anybody. I rented crutches and hobbled along. We camped out; I slept on the ground,

~ ~ ~ ~ ~ ~ ~ ~ ~ ~ ~ ~ ~ ~ ~ ~ ~ ~ ~

played with the children and tried to be a good sport.

But it was no holiday trying to get around with the inside of my knee in shreds. By the time we reached Southern Oregon, I was in so much pain I thought I would die, but I didn't. I added insult to injury when, in the middle of the night, deep in sleep, I kicked off my covers and woke up to the sound of my own screams. I had torn the shredded anterior cruciate ligament off the bone. But I still wouldn't quit. On the outside, I kept a smile on my face while I was scared to death on the inside, and was angry with my family for not recognizing my distress and stopping me. That afternoon, I joined everyone for a bone-bouncing stage-coach ride in historic Jacksonville, Oregon.

Finally, with the holiday over, we drove home, I in a panic because I knew something had to be done, and it wasn't going to be easy.

I went to see an orthopedic surgeon the next day. He agreed to operate to repair the damage. He later confessed that he was totally unprepared for the irreversible damage inside the knee joint. The prognosis didn't look encouraging. I told him I didn't care what it looked like; I would walk! I would walk on determination and will power, if I had to.

No matter how hard I tried, I couldn't walk.

Over the next few years, my leg gave way and I crashed to the floor countless times — on the street, in a store, at home. I'd pick myself up and try all over again.

Pride kept my physician from admitting that anything could have gone wrong, and he insisted my knee was just fine. The reason I couldn't walk, he pointed out, "is because you are neurotic." According to him, I didn't want to walk. I finally told him, "I may be neurotic — being crippled and in pain can make you that way — but I still can't walk!"

~ ~ ~ ~ ~ ~ ~ ~ ~ ~ ~ ~ ~ ~ ~ ~ ~ ~ ~ ~

There followed more surgery, new doctors, physical therapy, more complications, different opinions, sharp, dull, intermittent and chronic pain, heavy straight-leg casts — all of which would become part of my life for several years. It was terrible, a nightmare come true.

I still couldn't walk.

Finally, I found a doctor who, after examining me, said, "I don't know how you can stand on this leg, much less walk."

Flooded with relief, tears rolled down my face. Finally, here was someone who agreed with me and could fix it. Bolstered up by the confidence I had in my new doctor and my reassuring sense of competence in his ability, I underwent one more surgery which consisted of a totally new and radical procedure. Success! This time it worked.

After all the endless pain-filled years, my purple heroics of raising two young children and running a household from my bedside, I finally got better. I could use my leg without touching off a dazzling white agony of pain.

Lisa and Mark grew quite self-sufficient during those difficult years. Lisa could fix dinner by the time she was seven years old. Mark could make his bed and do laundry by the time he was five. It is amazing how — at any age it seems — we can rise to the challenges at hand and become better and stronger in the process.

Gary continued to earn good money, and we had built a monument to ourselves. By the age of thirty-five I had the perfect house, the perfect neighbors, the perfect life. Unfortunately, I still wasn't happy. Everyone and every-thing was too perfect, and I realized that I didn't want my children to grow up in this pure and rarefied atmosphere. There was a big world out there that was vastly different from the miniscule corner of sheltered living we occupied.

~ ~ ~ ~ ~ ~ ~ ~ ~ ~ ~ ~ ~ ~ ~ ~ ~ ~ ~ ~

I wanted the children to see more of the world. I wanted them to see people who had less, little or nothing, people who didn't speak English, people whose urgency lay in the need to do no more than feed themselves and keep a roof over their heads.

I wanted to expand their horizons and let them see a bigger world than their manicured backyard. I didn't want them to take our lifestyle for granted. I wanted them to appreciate their opportunities, but at the same time they needed to know that they had to earn their way. I wanted them to enjoy prosperity as a result of their efforts rather than believing it was owed to them. There was nothing like travel to achieve those things.

On top of all these noble concerns for my children's growth, my own needs could not be denied much longer. I had to get out of my pattern of living and set my feet on a new and different path. I couldn't wait any longer. It was time to take that trip around the world.

Somewhat apprehensive, I approached Gary with my suggestion. "We need to sell this house, take the money and join the Foreign Legion," I told him as matter-of-factly as I could one Sunday in the fall of 1975. My heart pounded in my chest. I felt my life depended on his agreeing to my seemingly outrageous scheme. Surely, he would see my point. My timing must have been perfect. Gary was burnt out at work and ready for a stimulating change.

To my delight and surprise, quiet, centered and dependable Gary went along with the idea — modified, of course. That bit about the Foreign Legion was too drastic. We agreed to sell the house, take the money, pack our bags and see the world.

We started tossing ideas around and discarding them as quickly. We finally settled on visiting South Africa for a

~ ~ ~ ~ ~ ~ ~ ~ ~ ~ ~ ~ ~ ~ ~ ~ ~ ~ ~ ~

while: the weather was good, the economy was steady, and English was spoken there. What more could we want? We were totally naive about conditions on the African continent and uninformed about the realities of Apartheid in Johannesburg. Consequently, we would have a big surprise waiting for us.

Our excitement grew as the plans for our upcoming adventure took shape. We would take time to get there, we decided. We wanted to see the world at our own pace and travel on a whim, go where and when at a moment's notice. We would travel light, free of schedules and disciplines. I wanted to experience my family, my world and myself in a different way, in another setting.

Gary quit his job, we sold our beautiful house, took the children out of school, packed one carry-on bag for each, and were set for adventure. For the second time in my life, I felt unencumbered and free to express myself without restriction, without shame. Even though our friends and family were horrified, I wasn't about to take no for an answer.

LIFE LESSONS

ONE WOMAN

When people tell you you can't do something, they are really telling you "they" can't do it. Many of our friends and family members are vested in our staying the same and keeping the peace. If we come up with a different and perhaps radical idea for change, we hear a million reasons why it won't work. While planning our trip, we were told

~ ~ ~ ~ ~ ~ ~ ~ ~ ~ ~ ~ ~ ~ ~ ~ ~ ~ ~ ~

we shouldn't take the children out of school and drag them halfway around the world.

Others admitted sheepishly they wished they could do it. My response was always the same: "You can do it. All you have to do is quit your job, sell your stuff, take your kids out of school, and go around the world."

Which is easier, staying with the status quo or expressing yourself in the fullness of who you are? Here are some thoughts for you to think about in a quiet place:

- ❧ Write down the dreams you had as a child.
- ❧ What are the themes of your childhood dreams?
- ❧ How many of these dreams have you actualized?
- ❧ Who tells you "No," and why? Do you tell yourself "No" most of the time?
- ❧ Begin today to visualize yourself in your dream. Do this every day until it is comfortable.
- ❧ What is the "essence" of your dream?
- ❧ How can you fulfill your dream right where you are?
- ❧ Tell someone your dream.

ONE LIFE

When you deny your truth and pretend, you not only shortchange yourself but everyone else.

We women tend to deny who we really are and pretend much of the time.

We pretend things are fine when they aren't. We pretend jokes are funny when they're not. We pretend the fellow in the office is not harassing us when he is. We pretend and pretend and pretend until we are so far removed from our real selves that we don't know who we are.

Generally we pretend to ourselves, which is the most

~ ~ ~ ~ ~ ~ ~ ~ ~ ~ ~ ~ ~ ~ ~ ~ ~ ~ ~ ~

damaging pretending of all. Sometimes it serves our purpose to pretend. It isn't so hurtful if we do it consciously rather than in unconscious self-protection.

I kept pretending there was something wrong with my head rather than my leg. That bit of pretending caused years of pain for my family and myself.

For the next month:

- Notice how many times you pretend during the day.
- Write down the circumstances.
- Write down an honest response for the next time.
- Visualize yourself unpeeling yourself like removing layers of skin from an onion until you reach the real you — your essence.
- Decide how you can be your authentic self right where you are right now. One day at a time.

THE MONEY MYSTIQUE

Pay cash for everything and live beneath your means, then you have options. You can take advantage of opportunities.

Most of us in these days of easy credit pay for something over and over again. The reason Gary and I could take our dream trip was because we had no debt. We live in a consumer society and are bombarded with 16,000 advertising messages a day. Don't be caught up in a frenzy of having "stuff." Be satisfied with what you have. I lived with TV trays as end tables for two years and didn't think anything of it. Don't think "stuff" buys happiness. Experiencing yourself to the fullest generates happiness.

We are told we will be happier, healthier, sexier if we

~ ~ ~ ~ ~ ~ ~ ~ ~ ~ ~ ~ ~ ~ ~ ~ ~ ~ ~ ~

have one thing or another. So we get it, but we don't feel better. So we think we need more. If we only had a certain symbol of success, we would feel better. We get it and we don't feel better. So we keep buying, trying to feel better, but we feel worse. Stop the cycle. Happiness comes from the inside out through understanding how we want to express ourselves and nurturing our souls, not through owning things.

For the next three months:

- ☞ Pay cash, do not use credit.
- ☞ Write down what you wanted to purchase with credit, but didn't.
- ☞ The following month, review the list and ask yourself "Am I less happy because I don't have "It?"
- ☞ If the answer is "Yes," then start putting money away so that you can have "It," and pay cash.

The problem with going into debt to buy consumer goods and services is that eventually you can't earn enough to make your payments. For example, suppose you decide to take a trip to Disneyland with your ten-year-old son. You don't have the cash to pay the $2,000 cost of the vacation, so you charge it on your credit card. Your creditor charges 18 percent interest for unpaid balances. You make the minimum payments. Your son is 21 years old before you have finished paying for that vacation. You have actually spent $3,960 for the experience. But the real kicker is you have to pay taxes on your money before you get it. So, if you are in a 28 percent federal tax bracket, you had to earn over $5,000 to pay the $3,960 for the $2,000 trip.

Ask yourself: Is paying interest to a bank or finance company a good use of your life energy? I have clients whose minimum consumer debt payments are more than 50

~ ~ ~ ~ ~ ~ ~ ~ ~ ~ ~ ~ ~ ~ ~ ~ ~ ~ ~

percent of their take-home pay. It takes years to climb out of a hole that deep. As a good friend said recently, "When you find yourself in a hole, quit digging."

If consumer debt is a problem for you, do the following:

- Make a chart of all your creditors. Include the amount owed, the minimum monthly payments, the interest rates. Give yourself a payment schedule, paying off cards with the highest interest rates first. Now consider this as debt and start paying it off as quickly as you can. Write down the date when you will be debt free. Keep a copy of the date in your wallet along with your credit cards. Visualize yourself as a person who pays her way as she goes.

- Don't use credit for anything that will be used up before you receive the bill. Use it only for long-term purchases such as a car or a computer.

- Give yourself milestones with rewards along the way. I have one client who has a chart on her bathroom mirror to show her progress. Every time she reduces her debt by $100, she puts a dollar bill on the chart. When the has $20, she has paid off another $2,000, and she treats herself to dinner out — and pays cash!

It is important to learn to use credit wisely, even while you are paying off your bills. So get a new credit card or use one you already have that doesn't have any balance due. Now use that card during the month and pay the entire balance due every month. You are in essence using it as a charge card, not a credit card. Don't be tempted to use this credit card unless you are certain you can pay the balance in full every month.

~ ~ ~ ~ ~ ~ ~ ~ ~ ~ ~ ~ ~ ~ ~ ~ ~ ~ ~ ~

Lenders are constantly telling us to use our home equity to bail ourselves out of debt. Don't be lulled into a false sense of security. You are just trading one type of debt for another. I have seen it time and time again where people feel so anxious and overwhelmed about their debt that they have to pay it off.

It truly may make sense to consolidate your debt by using the equity in your home. But not until you have learned to use credit wisely. I recommend you struggle along making minimum payments and using a credit card as a charge card until you are sure you have broken the debt cycle. Otherwise, you are in danger of feeling so good now that your credit cards are paid off that you start using them again. I know people who repeat this cycle every two or three years until their house is mortgaged to the hilt and they are once again maxed out on their credit cards. Their only alternative is to win the lottery or pray for an inheritance.

CHAPTER THREE

~ ~ ~ ~ ~ ~ ~ ~ ~ ~ ~ ~ ~ ~ ~ ~ ~

*"I am not the same having seen the moon
shine on the other side of the world."*
– *Mary Ann Radmacher-Hershey*

To this day, I am amazed we did it. I was thirty-five
and Gary was thirty-eight when we sold our fabulous house,
our status cars, our new appliances, lots of "stuff," and put
the rest in storage. We sold thousands of dollars' worth of
goods at garage-sale prices, and we were happy to do it. It
was a treat and a relief not to have so many things cluttering
up our lives. We took the money and ran. Mark was eight
and Lisa barely eleven when we took them out of school,
never letting their teachers know what we were about to do.
What could be more educational and enlightening than
travel? But I was afraid they would tell us "No."

Considering the length of our trip, we bought four big
suitcases. My father, a seasoned traveler, suggested we pack

~ ~ ~ ~ ~ ~ ~ ~ ~ ~ ~ ~ ~ ~ ~ ~ ~ ~ ~ ~

our new luggage with the things we intended to take, and carry them from our house down the hill to the supermarket to test how we would bear up under the load. The suitcases were a bust. Carrying those big monsters down was bad enough, but hauling them back up the hill sent me flying to the nearest store for one small carry-on piece of lightweight luggage and a couple of backpacks.

We said our hasty and teary goodbyes, and in May of 1976 boarded Pan Am's Spirit of Friendship flight to London. We were off on our adventure, to places we only had heard of and read about and experiences we had never dreamed about. We buckled ourselves into our seats, put on our headsets and fell quiet. Not one of us said a word. To this day, I wonder why not one profound thought came to my mind — all the way to England. I kept a little diary of our journey and whenever I want to revisit memories of the trip, I get it out. Many of the entries were directed to Gloria, a friend of mine whom I kept posted on our progress.

Gloria must have been amazed at our itinerary — or lack of one. We went all over the map — from the Alps to the Acropolis, from Europe to Capetown, from Rio de Janeiro to Venezuela, to sunny Curacao and Jamaica and back home again. From May to October we saw new and different things. We experienced the tragedy of the Soweto riots in South Africa, felt dwarfed by the mighty Alps and were deeply drawn to the ancient heart of Jerusalem.

In England, we did everything but visit the Queen. We delighted in the charm of the quaint villages in Spain, the antiquity of Greece and the exuberance of Italy. We gloried in the sparkling coastline of the Mediterranean, admired cathedrals, and the endless parade of paintings and sculptures. We saw the old and the new, compared traditions with the outcroppings of avant guarde notions, and went from

~ ~ ~ ~ ~ ~ ~ ~ ~ ~ ~ ~ ~ ~ ~ ~ ~ ~ ~ ~

one country to another, from one adventure to the next, wanting to remember it all.

London, England

Dear Gloria,

We've been gone for only five days, and it seems like a month. Gary is sick with strep throat, and our hotel is terrible. The shower gives us two, maybe three, drops of water at a time — makes washing your hair a real challenge. The food is awful. We are in mortal danger because the traffic comes zooming up on our left as we look right to cross the street. What the hell are we doing? Whose idea was it anyway to take an eight-year-old and an eleven-year-old and cart them off around the world? Once we lifted off in Portland, I had this sinking feeling that we were in big trouble. I intended to begin my travel journal with my profound thoughts about this adventure. Now I'm not sure what a profound thought is. Anyway, wanted you to know we made it this far and hope to survive.

Love,
Karen
xoxoxo

Copenhagen, Denmark.

Dear Gloria,

Danish pastries aren't what they are cracked up to be. The bakery is a big disappointment, but the country is cute and the schnapps is great. Everybody rides a bike and speaks English. We are staying in the private home of woman. She is the first woman the kids have seen who smokes a cigar. It's still pretty cold in Northern Europe. Wish we had brought warmer clothes. For now, we are stylishly attired in the layered look by wearing everything we brought with us at the same time. Rather stifling, but it lightens our suitcases.

Love,
Karen
xoxoxo

Nice, France

Dear Gloria,
France is beautiful. We have spent the last few weeks on the French Riviera. Mark goes down to the beach with his sand bucket and stops when he spots a topless woman. Then he calls for Gary to come help him. Gary came up with the idea. It's crude, but it works.

The bread is wonderful. We mostly picnic because the weather is great and we are on the go. We've visited Picasso's house near Antibe, Monaco and Cannes. I felt pretty tacky next to all the beautiful people in Cannes, and to make matters worse a bird pooped on my head. The same thing happened to me in Denmark and Holland, where Gary leaned over to me and whispered, "Would you be offended if I told you a bird just dropped doodoo on your head?" We laughed till we cried. My head must have target written all over it.

Love
Karen
xoxoxo

~ ~ ~ ~ ~ ~ ~ ~ ~ ~ ~ ~ ~ ~ ~ ~ ~ ~ ~ ~

Altafulla, Spain

Dear Gloria,

Here we are in Altafulla, Spain. What an adventure we had getting here. Don't really even know where it is, but the sea is beautiful and we are enjoying a welcome rest from our travels. Overheard a conversation between a Canadian and an Australian on a cruise up the Rhine River about this place, and here we are. It is a small, quaint village which apparently never hosted Americans with small children before. The first night when we walked into the dining room "Amazing Grace" was playing. I'll probably always think of this place whenever I hear that song.

We are well and looking forward to our next adventure. Don't know where we will go from here but will keep you posted.

Love,
Karen
xoxoxo

Rome, Italy

Dear Gloria,

In a hurry, but thanks for the letter. We picked up our mail at American Express this morning. It is fun to hear from people. Home seems very far away. We spent America's 200th birthday at a Fourth of July celebration hosted by the American Embassy on a hillside outside Rome. It was really fun to hear mostly English spoken for a whole day — great fireworks, too. But I guess the Italians invented pyrotechnics, didn't they?

~ ~ ~ ~ ~ ~ ~ ~ ~ ~ ~ ~ ~ ~ ~ ~ ~ ~ ~ ~

We're leaving for Greece in a few hours. We'll miss Italy. It is grand. The Italians sort of cornered the market on marble sculptures. The paintings aren't bad either.

Love,
Karen
xoxoxo

Sitia, Crete (Greece)

Dear Gloria,

Our room costs six dollars a night for the four of us and is probably overpriced! If our friends could see us now, they wouldn't believe we would stay in a place like this, yet it somehow seems okay. By contrast, we are hanging out with a Danish couple who live in a cave. The other day I mentioned to her how tan she is. In her wonderful Danish accent she replied, "Am I? I haven't a mirror, you know."

Mark's best friend is Alex, a fisherman who fishes right in the middle of the bay. Dark and swarthy, his toothless smile radiates love. He uses a huge string of hooks each embedded in a ball of bread for bait. He and Mark have caught some wondrous fish, including an octopus, which we cooked up at the restaurant — on a spit, no less. You should have seen the poor thing with its tentacles flopping round and round. We invited Alex and our other friends to join us. Could we just stay here where time stands still?

Hope you are well.

Love,
Karen
xoxoxo

~ ~ ~ ~ ~ ~ ~ ~ ~ ~ ~ ~ ~ ~ ~ ~ ~ ~ ~ ~

Jerusalem, Israel

Dear Gloria,

No feeling can compare to being right in the middle of the birthplace of several of the world's major religions — and the beginning of so much of man's history. We rode a camel on the hill above the city where Jesus ascended to heaven. The camel driver kept telling us Henry Kissinger rode the same camel. We couldn't understand his English until he opened his jacket and pulled out a ratty old copy of *Newsweek* with a picture of him and his camel with Henry.

Spent a day trekking up Masada overlooking the Dead Sea and actually stood in Herod's ballroom. Can you imagine standing in the same place King Herod stood?

Went to Bethlehem to the birthplace of Christ. Four religions share the Church of the Nativity. Amazing.

We visited the Tomb of the Patriarchs in Hebron and walked the Stations of the Cross to Calvary. You'll be disappointed to know the Station V bookstore has moved across town. Strange to see the modern world overlaid on antiquity.

In Nazareth, which still looks like an ancient city, "The Red River Valley" was blasting from a set of loudspeakers right outside the Church of the Annunciation. Nazareth looks pretty much to me like it must have in Jesus' time. At least the way it is portrayed in the movies.

We stayed the month because our friends, the Shenkars, are here and are being wonderful hosts. Beautiful country juxtaposed with history and hatred. Awesome!

~ ~ ~ ~ ~ ~ ~ ~ ~ ~ ~ ~ ~ ~ ~ ~ ~ ~ ~

Next stop South Africa. Hope it will be as
wonderful as we want it to be. I'll write soon.
Love,
Karen
xoxoxo

After a month's sojourn in Israel, where we met up
with good friends and filled ourselves with the sights and
sounds of that ancient land, we were ready to go on to South
Africa. We heard about the Soweto riots starting in June but
assumed they would be over by the time we got there.
However, when we checked in with the United States
Embassy in Israel, we were warned that travel to South
Africa was dangerous. We asked if we would have been so
warned had we declared our destination was Israel. The
reply was, "We would have told you the same thing. Travel
to Israel is dangerous."

We passed on Kenya because Idi Amin was terrorizing
that part of the Continent at the time, and we were not so
adventurous or foolish to get into the thick of it. Without
giving danger much thought, we jetted off to South Africa
one hot August night. We had residence visas, and Gary had
taken a brief fact-finding trip to Johannesburg the previous
January. We thought we knew what to expect. Wrong.

At first we were bothered by the fact we were given a
thirty-day visa — not a 365-day one. But after seeing the
appalling conditions apartheid imposed on the black people
of South Africa, a thirty-day stay seemed ample. We went to
the Fontana Discount Inn close to downtown Johannesburg
and settled in for our limited visit, determined to see as
much as we could before we had to leave.

~ ~ ~ ~ ~ ~ ~ ~ ~ ~ ~ ~ ~ ~ ~ ~ ~ ~ ~ ~

On our first night in Johannesburg, we went for a walk downtown to have dinner. What an experience! So many black skins, so few white ones. And we were white-white — the kind that glows in the dark. Mark was terrified, and Gary and I were pretty unnerved ourselves.

The park benches in Joburg Park were marked "Net Blankjes," for whites only. We went to a steakhouse someone recommended and ordered dinner. There were no blacks in the restaurant — except, of course, as help. Blacks were allowed to order food for take-out only, but were not allowed inside the restaurant. It was embarrassing to watch whites order blacks around in a less-than-civilized manner. Apartheid killed our enthusiasm for South Africa.

On the other hand, we liked the white people we met — they were regular guys! Although worried about the rioting, they wanted to keep the status quo. They balked at changes that threatened their life style as they knew it. They liked the way things were — after all, it had been like this since the day the first white man set foot on the Dark Continent.

I was doing our laundry in a Johannesburg laundromat on the day blacks were on strike and refused to come from Soweto into the city to work. I chuckled at the white women who came in to wash their own clothes — a chore blacks had been doing for years. These women grumbled loudly about the inconvenience. Many were in tears because they didn't know how to operate a simple washer and dryer. These women had all their housework done for them. It is no wonder they resisted the new ways.

~ ~ ~ ~ ~ ~ ~ ~ ~ ~ ~ ~ ~ ~ ~ ~ ~ ~ ~ ~

Johannesburg

Dear Gloria,

Emigration wouldn't let us stay because of the Soweto riots. The government gave us a short stay permit — I have a feeling it will be enough for me. Apartheid goes against all our values.

Mark was sick. I stayed with him in our room and had a chance to talk to the hotel maid. She is black and lives in Soweto. This morning, she was in tears. Her neighbors burned her kitchen the day before because she came into the city to work and didn't observe the strike. I feel so sorry for her.

In Capetown last week, we tried to board a bus for non-whites. It was sort of funny, sort of sad. We were trying to get on the bus, and the driver wasn't letting us, but didn't say it was because we were white. It took us a while to understand the deal. What a complicated way to live.

Sometimes I can't believe I am seeing what I am seeing. The other night we witnessed an African work himself up into a frenzy and pick up a railroad tie with his teeth. Happy we can't stay, but wouldn't have missed it for anything. Till the next stop.

Love,

Karen

xoxoxo

After two weeks in South Africa we took a flight on Bulowao Air destined for Rhodesia, now Zimbabwe. There were only six passengers on the plane — the four of us and two nuns. There may have been an element of danger involved, but I am glad we went. Nothing happened, except that we had a wonderful time. Immaculate huts with

~ ~ ~ ~ ~ ~ ~ ~ ~ ~ ~ ~ ~ ~ ~ ~ ~ ~ ~ ~

thatched roofs clustered in our picturesque resort village. The service was great because there were so few tourists. Each table was served by one waiter resplendent in full regalia with gold epaulets and red sashes. We felt a bit tense to see the military in camouflage fatigues secure the area at night — not a bit like Portland, Oregon!

We visited the game reserve of Wanke, where wild animals live in their natural habitat. It was an indescribable experience to watch a giraffe sprawled out over its long front legs drinking from a watering hole not ten feet away. We got drenched in the Rain Forest of Victoria Falls and didn't care. All in all, we couldn't get over the exuberant and exotic beauty of this magic land.

We didn't leave Africa without visiting Capetown, where we rode the cable car up Table Mountain to get a good look at the spot where the Atlantic and Indian oceans converge. What a beautiful place. There is an actual line where the two different-colored bodies of water meet. It still sings in my heart. Altogether, Africa was a wonderful experience. We made friends with everyone we met — black and white alike.

We knew we had to return home, but we weren't ready yet. Gary had called his former partner and told him he wanted to resume their business relationship. His partner replied with an enthusiastic "Great! We'll see you when you get here." We decided to take the long way home and spent another two months traveling. We didn't want our adventure to end.

~ ~ ~ ~ ~ ~ ~ ~ ~ ~ ~ ~ ~ ~ ~ ~ ~ ~ ~

Curacao,
Netherlands Antilles

Dear Gloria,

We will be home before we know it. The Caribbean is our last stop. Just left Bolivia and don't have to go back. Different, but no thanks.

Curacao is a darling little island. We met up with a guy named Tony, who took us all around the island on a day tour. It turned out poor Lisa is really sick. She didn't say much before we left the hotel that morning, but she got sicker and sicker during the day. To make matters worse, while visiting a sea cave, she raised herself up without realizing there was little headroom, and almost knocked herself out. I felt so badly about it.

Once back at the hotel, we managed to find a doctor. She had the flu. He wrote out a prescription, but it took Gary all night to have it filled. The only pharmacy open was in an old part of town. The pharmacist waited on everybody but him. He was the last person served and didn't get back to our room until midnight.

He had set out on foot and I was sure he had been killed — never to be heard from again. I was in tears when he finally arrived with a prescription written in Papiamento (the local lingo.) Even though we couldn't read it, Lisa got well quickly.

Will write again soon.

Love,
Karen
xoxoxo

~ ~ ~ ~ ~ ~ ~ ~ ~ ~ ~ ~ ~ ~ ~ ~ ~ ~ ~ ~

Nassau, The Bahamas
September 1976

Dear Gloria,

Now I'm so sick I can't believe it. I had a slight cold. and my eardrums hemorrhaged from the pressure of the plane landing in Nassau. Pain like I've never felt before. The customs official made me stand forever until the luggage arrived. He wouldn't let me sit down even though there was a chair right there.

After we checked in at a hotel, I went straight to the hospital. I was the only white person in the waiting room among hundreds of blacks. Mercifully, they took me first. I felt bad for going out of turn, but that quickly turned to despair when I had to wait five hours to get my prescription. I spent most of the week flat on my back. I think I'm better now, but I'm scared to fly to Miami tomorrow.

Wish me luck.

Love,
Karen
xoxoxo

Orlando, Florida

Dear Gloria,

We made it to Miami without a hitch. I'm feeling great. We rented a car and drove to Disney World. It's great to be back in the United States — we all four bent down and kissed the ground. I can't tell you how wonderful it feels to have things you can count on. Traffic regulated, hot water, toilet paper that doesn't feel like crêpe paper, and soft towels. What more can you want? Tears streamed

~ ~ ~ ~ ~ ~ ~ ~ ~ ~ ~ ~ ~ ~ ~ ~ ~ ~ ~ ~

down my face during the Presidents exhibit at Disney World. We really take democracy and our standard of living for granted.

We plan to go all the way from Florida to Boston to see the Bicentennial cities, including Washington, New York and Philadelphia. Perfect ending for our most magnificent adventure. See you in a few weeks.

Take care,
Karen
xoxoxo

I have always been glad we took our round-the-world trip. The naysayers were wrong. You *can* drag an eight-year-old and and an eleven-year-old all over the world. We traveled by the seat of our pants. For example, when we heard about a lovely spot in Spain, we went there on the next train. When the BMW factory in Munich was closed to the children, we checked our luggage at the train station. Carrying just two backpacks, we took off to visit mad King Ludwig's opulent castles. We didn't have a change of clothes for three weeks. We never knew where we would spend the night, but we usually managed to find a room. We slept on the train if we had to.

Even though travel had its challenges, I was in heaven. I had no schedules, no money worries. I wore no makeup, had no hairdo, and forgot all about manicures. I had no new clothes and no things to take care of. We were living on a whim, relying on our wits to get us out of our occasional scrapes. I loved it.

We met wonderful people who were entranced with Mark and Lisa. The children helped us see a different world

~ ~ ~ ~ ~ ~ ~ ~ ~ ~ ~ ~ ~ ~ ~ ~ ~ ~ ~

than the one we experienced. One hot summer day, we were racing up the Spanish steps in Rome, when a street vendor yelled out, "Hey, Marko!" Mark told us he met the man a week before at the Loggia in Florence, while we were exploring the Uffizi Gallery. Leave it to children to make friends.

I wondered just what they learned, what they would remember and what difference this big trip would make in their lives. They were so young, but I believe experiencing the world has had a major impact on their lives. You can read about Venice and how there are but a few cobblestone streets, and all traffic takes place on streets of water — the canals of Venice — but you can't know it until you live it yourself.

It is a great experience opening doors to other worlds and discovering the unique sights, sounds and traditions of foreign lands. I enjoyed listening to snatches of conversations from other travelers (English-speaking only), one of which comes to mind every time I think of Greece.

I overheard two matronly American women descending the ancient steps of the Parthenon on the Acropolis, complaining that the steep, uneven stones — worn away by the centuries — were not lined with rubber treads for easier walking! That would have been like putting jockey shorts on Michelangelo's *David.*

We were not the typical American tourists. We never paid more than twenty-five dollars for a room for the four of us. On Crete, a parade of ants descended from the ceiling of our six-dollar room for breakfast every morning like clockwork The spray from the shower was far reaching and drenched the rest of the small concrete communal bathroom. "If our friends could see us now." It wasn't the Four Seasons or the Ritz, but it was fun.

~ ~ ~ ~ ~ ~ ~ ~ ~ ~ ~ ~ ~ ~ ~ ~ ~ ~ ~ ~

We had quite a time — what a trip, what stories to tell, what memories! It was fun to trade in our security blanket of a lifestyle for a wild fling at the world. I know we got value for our money. Besides, money was never at the base of any of my life's concerns. I had an innate knowing about money that had something to do with how I felt about myself, my values and priorities. I always knew I could create the money to do whatever I wanted to do.

And it was money, and The Money Mystique, with which I would get totally involved. At the time I didn't have the faintest idea about my future or my career that would blossom much later in the financial canyons of New York City — without Gary.

But first things first. I would have to go home and face the fact that we would have to start all over again with what we had left in our bank account, in our emotional reservoir, and the storage unit that held our favorite possessions.

LIFE LESSONS

ONE WOMAN

As women, we often feel as though we aren't safe. Our life experiences teach us we need to be careful. Often we look to someone else for security. Yet, real security comes only from within. If you depend on other people or things to give you security, you can't fully express yourself because you function from a base of fear. Fear paralyzes you. It makes you do and say things that are not true to yourself. It is impossible for you to fully express yourself if you are fearful of your own power or fearful of another's

~ ~ ~ ~ ~ ~ ~ ~ ~ ~ ~ ~ ~ ~ ~ ~ ~ ~ ~

power over you. One of the keys to happiness and fulfill-
ment is to understand yourself and be secure in the
knowledge that you are responsible for yourself, and you
are up to the task. Once you feel that internal security, no
one or no circumstance can take it away from you. It is
yours for life.

Be secure in the knowledge of who you are, why you
are on this earth, and your special contribution. No one can
take your security away from you — you have to give it to
them.

On our extensive travels, I learned I could get myself
out of any jam, any time, any place.

Answer these questions:

- What does security mean to me?
- When do I feel secure? Why?
- When do I feel insecure? Why?
- Notice the patterns. Who is there? What are you
  doing? What are they doing? What can you do to
  change your feelings of insecurity?
- Meditate twenty minutes every day and focus on
  security and what it feels like.
- Talk with other women about their feelings of
  security and insecurity. How are you different?
  How are you the same?

ONE LIFE

The world is a big place with lots to learn and lots to
see. If we limit ourselves to what we already know, we miss
most of life's pleasures. Take time to stretch yourself
beyond your limits. It may feel risky, but life is to be
enjoyed and experienced. We will always have everything
we need.

~ ~ ~ ~ ~ ~ ~ ~ ~ ~ ~ ~ ~ ~ ~ ~ ~ ~ ~

Just for fun:

- Read a book about a place you've never been.
- Take a trip to a place you've always wanted to visit.
- Don't let anything stop you — children, partner, work, anything. This is your life and you need to experience yourself to the fullest. Maybe you need to wait for awhile, but set the intention and work towards the goal. You grow stronger with each success.
- Focus on where you feel successful, not on where you miss the mark.
- Stepping out is scary. Take baby steps at first.

THE MONEY MYSTIQUE

As Americans, we have this idea that we should have the comforts of home even when we are traveling. This idea can prevent us from truly seeing another country. I've always believed if you want to go to Rome and stay at the Hilton with other Americans, you might as well stay home.

There are scores of books written about traveling on a budget. I suggest you pick up one or two about a place you'd like to visit and read them, just for fun. You will have many more options available, if you are willing to sacrifice comfort in exchange for experience. If you are interested in traveling:

- Decide where you want to visit and when you want to go.
- Determine how much you are willing to spend. For example, our trip cost us about $25,000. We determined not to pay more than twenty-five American dollars a night for a room. We traveled

~ ~ ~ ~ ~ ~ ~ ~ ~ ~ ~ ~ ~ ~ ~ ~ ~ ~ ~ ~

without reservations ahead of time. We discovered most train stations and most airports had a
service for finding us the perfect little room for
the four of us. If they didn't, we always lucked
out by asking a taxi driver or somebody who
would help us.

⊗ Don't expect the same accommodations you are
used to in the United States. Often the bathroom
was down the hall, and we shared it with other
travelers. The plumbing usually wasn't up to par.
Sometimes we had to be very creative in the
bathroom.

⊗ Wear the same clothes day after day. There is
also a benefit in not carrying around a suitcase
full of dirty clothes. I washed our clothes in the
sink and rinsed them in the bidet. I hung them to
dry on plastic inflatable hangers. When we'd
walk in from dinner, it would look like a half-
dozen people were hanging from the ceiling.

⊗ Look for opportunities to spend less.
  ⊷ Find things to do that are free.
  ⊷ Eat lightly and carry a large bottle of
    water.
  ⊷ Picnic rather than go to restaurants.
  ⊷ Pick up magazines and newspapers you
    see lying around on park benches and
    trains. English-language publications are
    quite expensive.
  ⊷ Don't worry about your hair or makeup.
    The natural look is easy and cheap!

~ ~ ~ ~ ~ ~ ~ ~ ~ ~ ~ ~ ~ ~ ~ ~ ~ ~ ~ ~

➥ Take public transportation. We didn't rent a car the whole time. We found everyplace we wanted to see by public transportation or by using a taxi. And we had some hilarious moments as a bonus.

➥ Walk from place to place. You see more of the sights on foot.

➤ Start putting money away today for that special vacation you've always wanted. Don't even consider that you won't do it. If you have the desire and consistently put the money aside to follow this dream, you can't fail.

CHAPTER FOUR

~ ~ ~ ~ ~ ~ ~ ~ ~ ~ ~ ~ ~ ~ ~ ~ ~ ~ ~

"Be not afraid of life. Believe that life is worth living, and your belief will help create the fact."
 – William James

Returning home — back in the United States — was both exhilarating and distressing. We stayed with my sister, Anne, until we could settle into a house again. I felt out of place, out of touch and out of sorts. Anne had a lovely, big home with all the latest and best conveniences. The thing that bothered me the most was her well-equipped kitchen and her big sink equipped with a faucet which instantly delivered boiling-hot water.

During the months of our low-budget travels, I had become accustomed to the simple things. The four of us had lived in places a lot smaller than Anne's kitchen and had

~ ~ ~ ~ ~ ~ ~ ~ ~ ~ ~ ~ ~ ~ ~ ~ ~ ~ ~ ~

been content. The instant hot water gadget really disturbed me. How could I live in a country where people had acres of kitchen counters and instant boiling water at their fingertips? Whatever happened to a water kettle whistling its comforting song on top of the stove? The "instant hot" is still the symbol to me of the over-consumption so many Americans feel is their well-deserved birthright. To this day, Anne and I laugh about my overreacting to a time-saving gadget, a convenience — certainly not an outrageous luxury.

We lived out of our suitcases for several weeks until we found a house. I felt ambivalent on moving day, but it turned out to be wonderful. Our brand-new house was spacious and comfortable, and I must admit it was a pleasure to be able to spread out and find privacy behind closed doors. It was fun seeing all of our things again, even though I realized with a sinking feeling that "having things" meant having to take care of them. Our "stuff" controls us in so many ways. And as much as I appreciate beautiful things, I knew for a fact they were superfluous to my happiness. I remember holding two lovely amber alabaster birds in my hands. Their smoothness rested cool against my skin and, while I admired their beauty, I realized I would have to dust them for the rest of my life.

Before we left on our trip, I thought we sold too much; now I thought we kept too much. I've certainly lightened the load since. I don't buy anything unless I absolutely love it or truly need it. I am very careful except in my garden. I'm a sucker for any new plant that comes along. But my garden is where I truly express myself, so I put my resources, time, energy and money to create it just the way I want.

We eventually unpacked, settled in and started life anew. By chance or divine design, our new home was

~ ~ ~ ~ ~ ~ ~ ~ ~ ~ ~ ~ ~ ~ ~ ~ ~ ~ ~ ~

located in the same school district our children had left so unceremoniously at the beginning of our trip several months ago. It didn't occur to us this would happen. I rather nonchalantly registered Lisa and Mark for classes as if we were new to the area, hoping no one would mention their absence. It worked pretty well. When asked where they had been I casually offered my explanation. "We decided to advance their education and took them around the world."

My remark was usually greeted with a strained smile and a grim nod. As it turned out, all Mark missed was instructions on cursive writing, while Lisa had to catch up on fractions. The knowledge the children gained about our world — everything they experienced traveling in Europe, Africa and South America — could hardly compare to having missed a few classes they could easily absorb during the school year. When Mark's fourth-grade class studied the Bushmen of Africa, he was able to tell the class about his trip to Africa and produce his warthog tusk to prove it. Yet, surprising to me, the children rarely talked about their trip with their friends and classmates. Years later, they explained to me they felt out of place having had such worldly experiences. It played out as reverse peer pressure. They didn't want to be viewed as different.

While Gary and the children settled back into the familiar routine, I was still at sixes and sevens. I didn't know what to do with myself. It was difficult to relate to some of my friends and the way of life in the United States. I tried very hard to fit into the old patterns and failed. Seeing how difficult and Spartan life was for millions of people on other continents had changed me.

But even more than that, I had loved being me without any constraints or expectations. How could I go back to this life after I had truly experienced myself for the first time? I

~ ~ ~ ~ ~ ~ ~ ~ ~ ~ ~ ~ ~ ~ ~ ~ ~ ~ ~ ~

never recovered completely, but eventually I picked up my old ways just as Gary and the children had done. I played bridge, volunteered at the local science museum, and took care of my family. But no matter how busy I made myself, no matter what distractions came my way, there was a constant stirring within me that I could not deny. I knew I was missing something.

After several months, I decided I wanted to work outside of the house. I started to look around for a part-time job and answered a few ads for receptionist or secretarial work. I've always been a whiz at typing and, Lord knows, I love to talk. I was serious about working, but I also knew how I might appear to an interviewer. I have been accused of possessing a touch of giddiness which could be quite disarming. I could just hear the wheels going around in the mind of the person behind the desk with the accompanying refrain: "Here's another ditzy blonde; loaded down with jewelry, dressed in silk — bright colors. Expensive! I wonder if she's serious. How good is she going to be?"

Well, I didn't change my looks or me to please anyone because I really didn't need a job. I would remain true to myself and let that become my greatest asset. After a week or two of looking around, I answered an ad for a receptionist at a construction company. I applied and was hired. It turned out to be a humbling experience. The company's letterhead was goldenrod in color with black printing. Even though goldenrod is my least-favorite color, I could have overlooked it if I had been able to locate goldenrod correcting fluid. Each time I made a typo, I had to use whiteout, because the typewriter did not have a correcting feature, which was readily available. It was a disaster. And to compound matters, the adding machine only handled figures in thousands, while I worked with calculations in the

~ ~ ~ ~ ~ ~ ~ ~ ~ ~ ~ ~ ~ ~ ~ ~ ~ ~ ~ ~

million-dollar range. It wasn't much fun, and I kept asking for a new IBM Correcting Selectric typewriter and a decent adding machine.

Finally, in frustration, I hung a huge sign on the wall behind my desk that announced to the world at large that: "I am only as good as my equipment." Well, that got everybody's attention. My bosses laughed and told me to get what I needed.

About a year later, my brother-in-law decided to run for Congress and asked me to manage his campaign. I had never done anything like that before. So naturally I said, "Sure! Sounds like a great idea," and resigned my job with the contractor.

I had always been a politics junkie, and this was right up my alley. I threw myself into the challenges of the job with my usual energy and dedication. What a thrill! It was exhilarating. The blend of activities constantly brought me into contact with new people and triggered an onslaught of new ideas and daring strategies.

I remember when Ronald Reagan, who was running for president at that time, came to town. I picked up his advance team at the airport. As we drove into town and discussed Reagan's candidacy, I thought to myself, "That man doesn't have a chance in hell of being elected president." I was so certain he wouldn't make it, I didn't bother to listen to his speech at the Red Lion Inn that night; instead, I was out in the hall visiting with friends.

I completely discounted Ronald Reagan as a viable candidate. I thought he was a joke. So much for my political savvy.

During the heat of the campaign, Lisa celebrated her thirteenth birthday. In spite of the attention, the party and the presents, I sensed that something was not right with her.

~ ~ ~ ~ ~ ~ ~ ~ ~ ~ ~ ~ ~ ~ ~ ~ ~ ~ ~

I took her aside to find out what was going on. She cried and said that she couldn't understand why I had to work so hard.

I tried to explain to my daughter that with her growing up, becoming a teenager, and Mark not far behind, I wanted to start building a life for myself. I didn't want my children to grow up believing they had to somehow take care of me because the only job I had was being a mother. I didn't want them to think they had to be with me every minute of the day to fill my needs. I hugged Lisa close and said, "You are going to be experiencing your own life. Your friends will become more and more important to you. You're growing up — you're a teenager."

Lisa looked at me with a sorrowful half-smile and said, "I don't know how to be a teenager."

I had no idea how true that was until much later.

We were ecstatic that my brother-in-law won in the primary. It was such a fun night. Hundreds of supporters gathered around congratulating the candidate and each other. Clusters of red, white and blue balloons, passionate speeches and roaring applause filled the ballroom at the stately old Benson Hotel in downtown Portland. I felt so alive and was enthralled with the whole thing.

The day after the primary, my six-year-old nephew was asked in school what his father had won the night before. He thought and thought about it and finally replied, "Well, I think he won a whole bunch of balloons because the car was full of balloons this morning." Kids!

Even though I loved the campaign, I became quickly aware of its shortcomings. People looked for problems where none existed, and everything, every issue, was up for grabs as far as the media, the opposition and our supporters were concerned. There were those who called our campaign headquarters to say they were in favor of our bumper

~ ~ ~ ~ ~ ~ ~ ~ ~ ~ ~ ~ ~ ~ ~ ~ ~ ~ ~ ~

stickers, and their numbers were matched by those who hated them.

The extreme right wing of the Republican Party had just gained a foothold in Oregon's political arena at the time, and it turned out to be a nightmare trying to please everybody. If one was in favor of women's right to choose, one lost the far right. If one was in favor of banning abortion, there went the moderates. Interestingly enough, the Republican Party still faces the very same dilemma as I write this nearly twenty years later.

In the words of one political pundit, "I'd never get involved in politics — it's too political." I realized I didn't have the stomach for the games politicians play, and that running my brother-in-law's campaign would be a one-time event in my life. I wanted to learn all I could and make the most of it.

Immediately after the primary, I began working on our strategy for the general election. The incumbent may be considered unbeatable, but we were going to do our best to get our candidate elected. People flew in from the National Republican Committee. We huddled all day. It was a high I'll never forget. We were on a roll.

Two days later, Gary sat me down and gave me the facts as he saw them. I had just walked in late for dinner again. I was higher than a kite, jabbering on about my day and the campaign. Gary averted his eyes, looked the other way and said, "I don't want you working on the general election. You know I'm having problems with my job and I need you here to support me. You have to quit before you get too involved. You aren't indispensible. They can find someone else — probably somebody better than you. Someone with experience."

I felt like he had kicked me in the stomach. For the

~ ~ ~ ~ ~ ~ ~ ~ ~ ~ ~ ~ ~ ~ ~ ~ ~ ~ ~ ~

second time in our marriage, Gary was saying, "You've made your bed, now lie in it." I didn't like that at all, but I felt I had no choice, and resigned my job with the campaign.

I didn't protest, even though I was hurt. I dutifully gave in to my husband's demands and went back to being wife and mother. Each time I jumped out of my designated circle in order to express *me* — my own self — address *my* needs, test *my* abilities and consequently have the chance to express myself, I was brought into line. Just mention the words wife and mother to me and self flew out the window. Who did I think I was? Bella Abzug? I felt bound and gagged, but I uttered not a word of protest, with one exception.

I asked Gary to pay me for staying home. I wanted him to match the few hundred dollars I would have earned running the campaign. Funny thing — it didn't fly!

I was back to being a full-time homemaker with no income. I suppose there was nothing wrong with my life, I just wanted more. Running errands, keeping house, fixing meals left part of me feeling unfulfilled and empty. I did however, spend a lot of "quality time" in my car ferrying the children to and from allergy shots, orthodontist visits, baseball practice. I loved being with them. And I truly loved keeping the house beautiful. My home was always a source of joy to me.

I had ignored my damaged knee during my trip, and it was not getting any better. My doctor recommended surgery and said that he would do the best he could with what was left of it. He gave me a fifty-fifty chance of recovery. If it didn't work, I would have to go to Texas for artificial

~ ~ ~ ~ ~ ~ ~ ~ ~ ~ ~ ~ ~ ~ ~ ~ ~ ~ ~

ligament replacement surgery. Worst case: I'd have another operation six months after I'd healed from the first one. Best case: I'd face a long recuperation process full of pain, helplessness and the frustrating chore of having to learn to walk all over again.

On a cold and rainy day in January of 1979, I met my sister Anne for lunch at a fancy restaurant with trendy food and cheeky waiters. We were looking good — dressed to kill, still young, pretty, slender and self-assured. We always had the best time, laughing at the world and ourselves in it. Our ability to laugh at ourselves is our greatest strength. There isn't a situation I've not laughed my way out of, eventually. At that time our lives ran almost parallel: Anne was about to be operated on for a lung condition, and I was facing another knee surgery. Neither Anne nor I were real keen on our husbands at that time, and the future didn't look rosy for our marriages. Yet, to look at us, no one could have guessed that we had a care in the world.

I never forgot Anne's comment. She said with a smile in her voice, "We may look great, Karen, but I have this feeling we're about to hit the skids." She was just turning forty-one, and my thirty-eighth birthday was around the corner.

Truer words were never spoken. Both our operations were horrendous, recovery time difficult and, to top it off, within two years we were both single.

My surgery was delayed for months because of a pesky staph infection in my ankle which just wouldn't budge. I soaked the offending joint in a tub of water three times a day from January till the end of April. I had the cleanest feet in town by the time I had my operation.

The day I walked into the hospital, I wondered how long it would before I could walk again. I vividly remember

~ ~ ~ ~ ~ ~ ~ ~ ~ ~ ~ ~ ~ ~ ~ ~ ~ ~ ~

lying on the gurney in the holding area for the longest time
waiting to go into the operating room. I wondered what the
outcome would be. How bad would it hurt? How long
would it take to heal? Would I ever get better?

The next time I saw my surgeon, he was at my
bedside, gently leaning over me and saying tearfully, "I
think we got it." Later he told me that my knee could last
anywhere from six months to twenty years. So far, so good
— it's been seventeen years now, and I'm still walking
without a limp.

The recovery was horrible. In order to reconstruct my
leg, they drilled, hammered and sawed. They clipped,
snipped and tucked. You'd think they were building a house,
not repairing a human joint. To top it off, I opted for a local
anesthetic because I generally flunk recovery-room
conduct. Never again!

Here a surgical team was doing unmentionable things
to my body and they were talking about playing golf in
Florida. I was furious and confused. Fortunately, I was
sedated enough I couldn't utter even the most inane
gibberish. However, when the doctor was casting my leg, I
made him cut it down in the crotch so it wouldn't jam into
my body every time I bumped my leg. That saved me from
bruising myself continually.

Compared to this operation, my previous ones were
kids' play. I was in monstrous pain. I felt like someone had
pulled my leg joint apart and placed the Grand Coulee Dam
on it. A friend of mine visited me in the hospital, but I was
hurting so badly that I kept my eyes shut and did not
respond to her presence. She bent over, kissed me on the
forehead and tiptoed out, believing I was sound asleep.

Time stood still. I was in a full leg cast for eight
weeks, which was followed by physical therapy. What a

~ ~ ~ ~ ~ ~ ~ ~ ~ ~ ~ ~ ~ ~ ~ ~ ~ ~ ~

treat that was! I worked on my leg from dawn to dusk. I was told to go home after the therapist got through with me, but I couldn't. I had to learn to walk. I worked with weights and the stair-stepper with tears streaming down my face. I walked on my toes and I walked on my heels. Sometimes I thought I'd never, ever walk again. The road before me stretched endlessly into a nebulous future that held no promises.

Eventually — months of agony and gallons of tears later — I walked again. It had been worth all the agony, the pain and the worry.

Several years later, my doctor confessed that he had never performed another surgery like the one he did on me. "No one but you," he remarked, "would ever have gotten out of bed again."

I have made the best of it. I've climbed Machu Picchu and the Himalayas. I've trotted all over Manhattan on this leg. From time to time I go in for a 10,000-mile checkup, where the doctor cleans out powdered bone and other extraneous materials using an arthroscope. I still fall down from time to time, but it isn't a bother.

To keep myself going and my mind away from the slow and torturous healing process that followed an operation, I studied something I always wanted to know about. After the first operation, I took up piano. I would sit at the piano for hours with my leg in its big cast sprawled awkwardly beside me on the bench. Eventually I could play Malaguena and Rhapsody in Blue rather well, I thought.

The second time around, I studied gems and and jewelry, giving a fleeting thought of becoming a gemologist — fleeting it was! During the last recovery, I studied nutrition. I researched the subject, read everything I could lay my hands on and, together with my sister Anne, wrote a

~ ~ ~ ~ ~ ~ ~ ~ ~ ~ ~ ~ ~ ~ ~ ~ ~ ~ ~

book, titled *The Leaner Look Book.*

I enjoyed the process and the challenge of developing ideas and seeing them completed. Anne and I had been in business together in the past, and we always had a good time. We sold our book all over the Northwest. It had been a new experience for both of us.

During my recovery, Gary decided to sell his interest in his home construction business and strike out on his own. Success is most often determined by timing, and Gary's couldn't have been worse. Interest rates had soared out of sight, and money was more than tight. Even though he rented an office, Gary spent a lot of time at home because he really had nothing to do. To quote someone's famous words, "I married for better or worse, but not for lunch."

It drove me crazy to have him in my territory at all hours. He turned out to be helpful around the house, but I resented having to fight him for who would get to fold the laundry. It was clear that he wanted me to be at home. Now, he was going to be at home too, trying to do my job. I wanted him to find something new to do, but he was determined to stick it out and wait for a change in the economy.

In the meantime, Phil Donahue and his feminist guests were raising my consciousness, and I could no longer deny what was happening to women and close my eyes to the career opportunities that were popping for them like rabbits out of a hat. Enlightened women were relentlessly delivering their messages of change and growth to women from coast to coast. Bras were burning in Dallas. When I caught Marilyn French, author of *The Women's Room* on the Donahue show, I ran out and bought her book immediately.

I was reading *The Women's Room* in the car waiting for Lisa to finish her visit with the orthodontist. I didn't

~ ~ ~ ~ ~ ~ ~ ~ ~ ~ ~ ~ ~ ~ ~ ~ ~ ~ ~ ~

notice her get in next to me, until she asked me politely, "Are we ever going to leave, Mother?" I reluctantly laid down the book and drove home, deep in thought. The book changed my life forever.

In jest, I have always accused Phil and Marilyn of having destroyed my life — as I knew it.

You know how you hear a message again and again, but then, suddenly, you know the message is for you. It's time to wake up. It feels like you've never really heard the words before, but suddenly you can't see over it, under it or around it — you have to go through it!

There is a section in *The Women's Room* I'll never forget. It was a message for me and became my personal wake-up call: The heroine in the book is head over heels in love with her man, who joins her at the breakfast table. She's chagrined to notice that his toenails need clipping and his robe needs washing. Next, the unthinkable happens. He opens his mouth and, "...suddenly, beloved said something stupid."

That line stayed with me — it's all about disillusionment. All of a sudden, I felt disillusioned about playing the same role, the same game in the same old way. I just couldn't do it anymore.

It was Superbowl Sunday 1980, and we were watching "the game" with several close friends when, without forethought, I leaned over to a friend of mine and whispered to her: "I'm going to go to work."

I didn't know that I had made a life-changing decision. I just thought I was going to get a job.

~ ~ ~ ~ ~ ~ ~ ~ ~ ~ ~ ~ ~ ~ ~ ~ ~ ~ ~

Life Lessons

One Woman

Up to this point, I spent my life in service to others — my parents, my husband and my children. I played a prominent role in their lives. I tried so many times to find a way to express myself, to discover who I was within the context of these roles, but it never worked. I felt that I had to betray everyone in order to be me, and it wasn't worth it — they were more important than I was. I didn't want to hurt or disappoint anybody. Yet, I felt alone and dissatisfied. Today, I realize that I was full of unexpressed anger, both at myself and my family.

The women of my generation were caught between the fifties model and the rapidly emerging women of the seventies. So many of us were confused, unappreciated and unfulfilled.

I encourage you to step outside yourself and examine the choices you are making.

- ◈ Write down what you believe your roles are.
- ◈ Categorize them by themes.
- ◈ Which of these roles makes you happy and complete?
- ◈ Which make you feel constricted and unfulfilled?
- ◈ List how you can feel more fulfilled in each role.
- ◈ How would you like to play each role? What needs to change?
- ◈ List five ways to make these changes and the consequences you foresee for each action.

~ ~ ~ ~ ~ ~ ~ ~ ~ ~ ~ ~ ~ ~ ~ ~ ~ ~ ~ ~

ONE LIFE

So far, my life was full of fun, adventure, pain and duty. At the tender age of thirteen, I knew I wanted to live in New York and see the world. An avid reader, I wanted to experience the fullness life had to offer. I kept trying to express myself within the periphery of my marriage, but the shackles were too tightly bound. The fact remained that, until I read *The Women's Room,* I didn't know I had the right to my own reality. I believed my dreams were just for dreaming.

- Find a quiet place and take the following:
    - A journal
    - Brightly colored pencils
    - Scissors, glue or tape
    - Magazines and pictures of things you love, people portraying activities and situations you want for yourself, and words that express your feelings.
- Draw a picture or assemble a collage titled: "My Right to Have" — include in your art:
    - your body,
    - your home,
    - your family,
    - your business
    - your finances.
- What does this picture say about you?
- Compare this picture to your life.
- Can you make better choices for yourself, given your better self-understanding?
- What are the consequences — best and worst?

~ ~ ~ ~ ~ ~ ~ ~ ~ ~ ~ ~ ~ ~ ~ ~ ~ ~ ~ ~

THE MONEY MYSTIQUE

Taking time out to recuperate from my surgeries gave me the gift of quiet and solitude. I looked at it as an opportunity to examine my life and the way I was spending my precious life energy. I thought about prosperity and abundance. We live in such an abundant Universe, yet we often feel so lacking.

Prosperity isn't about having money. It is about having the ability to express ourselves in the fullness of who we are. Many of us have a poverty consciousness about relationships, work, money, and life in general. We envy others for their special gifts or their bank account. We don't truly understand we can use our special gifts to create the bank account we desire.

We reach adulthood with jaded attitudes about money. Most of us don't have very good role models in our families of origin about money and how to use it with joy and creativity. We observed conflict around money and how one person or another used it.

Those of us who were raised post-World War II were raised in the Golden Age of Consumption in America. We were led down the Madison Avenue path that consumption brought happiness. And this just isn't true. But once we are caught up in the myth, it is hard to break out. And having easy credit makes it more difficult than ever.

Yet, poll after poll confirms that Americans are less and less satisfied with their lives, while consuming more and more goods. There is a rainbow on the horizon. All across America there are people who are practicing voluntary simplicity. They believe more isn't necessarily better. They are choosing to express themselves through

~ ~ ~ ~ ~ ~ ~ ~ ~ ~ ~ ~ ~ ~ ~ ~ ~ ~ ~ ~

means other than having the latest big-screen TV or the newest high-priced car. You can practice voluntary simplicity yourself.

- ☞ Buy a book about simplifying your life, both physically and spiritually.
- ☞ Look around you to see what you own that truly brings you happiness.
- ☞ List all the things you own that you don't really want or need.
- ☞ Resolve to ask yourself, "Do I want it or need it?" before you buy.
- ☞ Enjoy the freedom that comes with giving up your addiction to more, better and bigger.
- ☞ Enjoy a new, improved lifestyle and keep more money in your pocket for that special vacation or for your future.

I've always gone overboard at Christmas, buying and buying until the last store closed the day before the big holiday. There were just too many bargains to pass up! The past two years, I've taken $300 in one-hundred-dollar bills shopping with me. I decided this was the maximum I was going to spend. I've gone from store to store, shopping for each person on my list and paying cash. When the $300 was gone, I was finished with my shopping. There were three major benefits:

1. I didn't have any Christmas bills to pay in January.
2. I could enjoy the holidays more because shopping played a very small part in the celebration.
3. Christmas was more fun because we spent our time in fellowship rather than opening presents.

~ ~ ~ ~ ~ ~ ~ ~ ~ ~ ~ ~ ~ ~ ~ ~ ~ ~ ~ ~

You could try something like it for your next major gift-giving extravaganza.

CHAPTER FIVE

~ ~ ~ ~ ~ ~ ~ ~ ~ ~ ~ ~ ~ ~ ~ ~ ~ ~ ~

"It is not because things are difficult that we do not dare; it is because we do not dare that they are difficult."
– Seneca

I wanted to go to work. Just making that decision felt good — even exciting. I was eager and ready to learn new things, to have a new adventure and an opportunity to go beyond the confines of home and family. I had spent the past seventeen years in suburbia, and it was time to get out into the business world — time for me to get a real job downtown. I knew nothing about the business of business, but that didn't worry me. I was chomping at the bit to find out. I also knew that I had to focus on the "what" and not on the "how." Once I had the "what" in place, the "how" would take care of itself.

~ ~ ~ ~ ~ ~ ~ ~ ~ ~ ~ ~ ~ ~ ~ ~ ~ ~ ~ ~

Lisa was almost fifteen and Mark was thirteen. Their lives were headed in new and different directions, leaving me behind. What would I do when they were gone? It made sense to prepare myself for the time when my nest would be empty, with the possible exception of Gary.

I didn't say much to him about my intentions of going to work, while I quietly planned my strategy. I was in no mood to be told "No" this time. My turn had come, and I was going to take it. The brass ring had been beyond my grasp too many times, and I was not about to get off the carousel. The matter was not up for discussion, and I didn't really want to know how Gary felt about my working. I knew there would be a confrontation; I would not back down. I downplayed the matter within the circle of my family as much as possible and continued my life in the slow lane at home.

It took me just a week to get ready to look for a job. First of all, I needed a résumé. What could I say about work experience? I managed a home, raised two children, did volunteer work, cooked, cleaned, worked part time, painted, grew wonderful flowers, carpooled, knitted, sewed, and what? I had done all that for almost two decades, which didn't make me the ideal candidate for blazing a trail in the business world.

I could make up for the lack of career activities by just being me: eager, enthusiastic and confident. I happily put together a credible résumé and, come to think of it, I looked good on paper. I'd written a book, managed a congressional campaign and worked for a construction company. It could have been worse.

I was ready to take on the world — or Portland, Oregon, to be specific. The day after my thirty-ninth birthday I started my job hunt. I dressed in my one and only

~ ~ ~ ~ ~ ~ ~ ~ ~ ~ ~ ~ ~ ~ ~ ~ ~ ~ ~

suit — a short black wool jacket over a slim skirt, a white blouse, black city pumps, and just a discreet touch of jewelry. I had read the latest dress-for-success book and knew not to appear frivolous. I drove my station wagon downtown, parked in an all-day lot and started pounding the pavement.

It was easy, nothing to it! I picked the nearest big office building, started on the ground floor, and called on every office on every floor. I asked for the employment department (before it was called the personnel department or human resources) and filled out an application. Even though most of the time there were no openings, I completed the necessary paperwork. Just in case a position became available, my name would be on file.

I even applied for jobs in places I didn't like — I wouldn't have taken a job if they offered me one. I just wanted the experience of filling out the application, having a conversation with the people in charge, and getting the general feeling of what these businesses were all about. I enjoyed meeting different people and encountering different commercial enterprises offering a variety of opportunities. I was amazed at the many kinds of positions and career possibilities available, and thought it fun being a part of it all. I was shopping for a job, and I would keep on shopping until I found exactly what I wanted.

Looking for work became a routine. Every Tuesday, Wednesday and Thursday, from ten o'clock in the morning until four in the afternoon, I was downtown pursuing my quest. Two friends of mine owned a small boutique, called Sandra's, in the heart of the city, and I made their place my "Operation Job Search" headquarters. I'd stop by for coffee about nine in the morning, chat about what I intended to accomplish that day, report back about lunchtime, and recap

~ ~ ~ ~ ~ ~ ~ ~ ~ ~ ~ ~ ~ ~ ~ ~ ~ ~ ~ ~

my day later in the afternoon. I had to be at home at a
certain hour to carpool and fix dinner.

My friends had the best time listening to my antics —
they laughed at my reports and actually looked forward to
my dropping in. There's nothing like having good friends on
your cheering team. They couldn't believe my audacity in
approaching job situations and, frankly, neither could I. I
honestly felt no fear and had a lot of fun.

Several weeks flew by. I enjoyed excellent responses
to some of the applications I had filled out and left scattered
about town, like confetti at a party. I laughed and talked
myself into the executive suites of nearly every company,
which I found absolutely exhilarating. I was in demand. It
cracked me up. Sometimes a company would bring in a vice
president or senior officer to look me over and convince me
to take their job offer. It was quite flattering, to say the least,
and I had a great time.

It occurred to me that I was having more fun looking
for a job than I would probably have getting one. The
problem with getting a job is the fact that your boss expects
you to come back the next day and the day after that. But
while I was looking for a job I could come and go as I
pleased. I also realized with total wonder and delight that I
could be anything I wanted to be. I could pick and choose
the best job for me. That was news to me, and good news at
that.

I decided to put a price on my head and make the job
hunt worthwhile. I wanted an income of $25,000 a year.
When I told my downtown friends I was going to make that
kind of money, they doubled over with gales of laughter. By
then my job search had become a small happening at the
dress shop — almost the event of the day. Even several of
the women customers got in the act and inquired how my

~ ~ ~ ~ ~ ~ ~ ~ ~ ~ ~ ~ ~ ~ ~ ~ ~ ~ ~

project was going. One friend of mine humored me with a pat on the back and a jolly, "Why don't you just do that, Karen." I joined in the merriment, giggled and roared, but deep down, I just knew it would happen. I would get a position that paid me $25,000 — just wait and see.

This wasn't about the money. I always looked at money in a different light than most people. I always had enough money, and never experienced lack. When I had money, I spent it. When I didn't have money, I didn't. Simple. I would always have enough money — always. I knew that.

I remember losing my billfold in the eighth grade. I came home from a bus trip to Salt Lake City and it wasn't in my pocket. I was devastated. Everything I had earned that summer was in that billfold. For three long, hot months I took care of three children from six o'clock in the morning to six at night. I cleaned the house, I ironed heavy, stiff army shirts for the children's father, all for the glorious sum of ten dollars a week. I was saving the money to buy my school clothes for the ninth grade. I didn't get any new school clothes that year. Perhaps that was one of the most important lessons I ever learned: I realized ultimately I would always have to take care of myself. Maybe that's why I always put money away for the future and don't carry it all around in my wallet.

Walking around Portland, I wasn't looking for my lost billfold anymore. I was looking for a job that would pay me $25,000 a year. My logic told me I was crazy. My intuition told me I could do it. If I am looking for that kind of a job and believe I will find it — it is there.

By the middle of March, I had called on practically every large company in the area: banks, retailers, insurance companies, law firms — you name it, I'd been there. I had

~ ~ ~ ~ ~ ~ ~ ~ ~ ~ ~ ~ ~ ~ ~ ~ ~ ~ ~ ~

the routine down pat. I'd walk into the employment office, fill out an application, and wait to see what would happen. I would usually be whisked into an inner office, where another meeting or a battery of tests had been arranged. At first I was scared to take these strange tests. In those days employers tested your personality to see if you were crazy, and they tested your ability to poke round pegs into square holes to see if you could think logically. I often felt crazy and illogical, but I passed their tests with ease.

I'd do better on some tests than on others, but most often I got to go for the next round. I felt like a contestant on the $30,000 Pyramid. The goal was to get to the next level, get the job offer. Then the choice was mine to take it or not. I wanted it to be my decision, not theirs.

Meanwhile, at home, I said little about my adventures in the city. Gary kept asking me when I would take one of the jobs I had been offered. To this day, I don't really know what his feelings were about my daily ritual of job hunting. I remember having a hard time explaining that none of the positions offered was the right one for me, and that the salaries were not near the amount I envisioned so clearly. I wanted a job that paid me $25,000. Soon the subject became a sore point at home, and I avoided talking about it, and without much fanfare I just kept looking for that big-bucks job. It had to be there!

One day I answered an ad in *The Oregonian.* It sounded interesting: "Prominent attorney looking for person to manage small law firm. Must have experience. College degree required."

I knew I could do that! After all, I had applied for so many jobs that I felt I had acquired "experience" by osmosis. When it came to the college degree — well, I would have to skirt that issue.

~ ~ ~ ~ ~ ~ ~ ~ ~ ~ ~ ~ ~ ~ ~ ~ ~ ~ ~ ~

However, I had no clue what qualifications and background were necessary to manage a law firm. I talked my way through the first interview with the professional recruiter who was conducting the job search. I wanted that position and was wracking my brain how I could convince her to hire me without experience. I must have done a good job because she recommended I meet with the attorney. (That recruiter is still one of my best friends.) As it turned out, she gave me a start in business, and I returned the favor a few years later by introducing her to a company that propelled her career to new heights.

As I was getting ready for my interview with the attorney, I had this feeling that This Was It! I dressed with great care for my first interview with "JBN." By then I had three suits and could go on several interviews with the same company without wearing my "one-and-only." That morning I chose a soft cream-colored suit and matching silk blouse, pearl earrings, and bright polish on my perfectly manicured nails. I was on my way — success, here I come!

When I arrived at the law firm, I timidly opened the door to the twelfth-floor suite of offices in the beautiful Benjamin Franklin Plaza building. I stepped into a quiet but plush surrounding with luxurious Wedgwood-blue Oriental rugs on highly polished floors. I almost panicked because I knew this was it — this would be my new beginning.

I immediately liked the man who greeted me with an easy smile and a firm handshake. He was of medium height with spare hair swooped over one side to cover his balding pate. I knew we'd get along.

He talked to me about his firm, and I understood approximately every other word he uttered. Yet, I nodded as if I knew what he was talking about. He must have been fooled and asked me come back in two days. I was

~ ~ ~ ~ ~ ~ ~ ~ ~ ~ ~ ~ ~ ~ ~ ~ ~ ~ ~ ~

delighted, even though a small voice protested with a worried, "Karen, what are you doing? You don't know anything about this. Are you out of your mind?" But I was so determined to get this job, I didn't pay any attention to my inner fear.

We met on three different occasions over the next ten days. It seemed the interviewing process would never come to an end. The third meeting took place over lunch on a Wednesday. The attorney put down his fork, pushed his plate to the side, carefully folded his napkin, and announced he would let me know his decision on Friday. What he didn't know was that I had decided to call a halt to my safari and take a job with an insurance company as assistant to the CEO and had promised I would call them by the end of day with my decision.

I stabbed at the remains of my lunch with my fork, moved the broccoli from here to there on my plate until I couldn't contain myself any longer. My back was to the wall, because I didn't want to work at the insurance company; I wanted this job. I felt my face turning a bright scarlet as I turned to JBN and quite unceremoniously blurted out, "I suggest you hire me right now and pay me $25,000 a year — otherwise, I'm making other plans."

There! I've said it. Take it or leave it.

After a brief but pregnant pause, he took off his glasses and placed them on the table as gently as if he were handling a precious piece of Waterford crystal, rubbed his eyes, looked at me and made a sound that resembled a repressed sigh. I thought my stomach would leap out of my throat when he smiled and said, "How about $24,000?"

A warm glow spread clear through me. But keeping an implacable straight face, I managed to utter a brief, "Close enough. When do I start?"

~ ~ ~ ~ ~ ~ ~ ~ ~ ~ ~ ~ ~ ~ ~ ~ ~ ~ ~ ~

Done. My search was over. I had held out for what I wanted, had accomplished what I set out to do, and was on my way to an altogether new and different life. Good for me; I could hardly contain my feelings.

I couldn't wait to get back to my friends at Sandra's. I bounced into the shop full of unmasked enthusiasm and victory tinged with a good dose of disbelief. "I did it! I did it!" was all I could yell several times, arms in a touchdown mode. I calmed myself long enough to sit down and report word for word the event that took place at lunch. When I finished, no one said anything for a brief moment. Then Sandra turned to me and asked with raised eyebrows, "How did you have the nerve to ask for that kind of money?"

My best friend, Karen, laughed, shook her head, questioning me, "How could he possibly pay you that much to manage his law office? You don't know anything about it."

Almost in tears of fright at that point, I mumbled, "I don't know. Oh, you guys, what am I going to do? I don't know the first thing about law. I'll be working for a securities attorney and I don't know what "securities law" is all about. Jesus! I've got a lot of learning to do, don't I?"

With that I quickly left my friends, ran to my car and raced home. I felt safe — maybe for the last time.

I started my job as office manager the following Monday. I woke up early with a good case of the jitters that morning. My heart was beating wildly while I was getting dressed and ready to leave the house. Questions, doubts and a case of sheer terror gripped me. What had I talked myself into? What was I going to do? How long would it take my new boss to find out I didn't know the first thing about the practice of law or the securities business? I didn't even want to think about the fact that I had no management experience.

~ ~ ~ ~ ~ ~ ~ ~ ~ ~ ~ ~ ~ ~ ~ ~ ~ ~ ~

I looked in the mirror, made a face at my image, and gave myself a quick lecture that went something like this: "What the hell, Karen! It's easier to start at the top and go down than to start at the bottom and crawl your way up. Besides, you're too old to work your way up — you've got to start at the top. Give it your best shot! Nothing ventured, nothing gained." End of lecture.

I had a fleeting thought about my telling e-v-e-r-y-b-o-d-y I knew about my good fortune and considered briefly the soul-searing embarrassment I would encounter if I failed. I'd cross that bridge if.... I grabbed my purse and ran out of the house, wishing for a split second I could change my mind. It might be safer if I could dig in the garden, knit, paint, or whatever. That moment too, passed in a flash. I was excited, I was on my way to managing the law offices of a prominent attorney, and heaven help me!

Driving into the city and parking my car had become second nature to me in the last three months, only that morning I became a member of the rush-hour set, and it took a bit longer to get downtown.

I talked to myself all the way to the city and up the elevator. I couldn't believe I was entering a whole new world. I really wanted it to go well. I had been introduced around to the other attorneys and support staff on my previous visits and felt pretty comfortable walking in.

I held onto the doorknob for support for just a moment, closed my eyes, took a deep breath, opened my eyes, gave the door a forceful push and breezed in as if I did this every day.

Leslie, the receptionist, a tall, blonde, rather gangly young woman, was less than cordial in her greeting. She was preoccupied with looking at a set of rather large photos of her wedding that cluttered up her desk. These pictures

~ ~ ~ ~ ~ ~ ~ ~ ~ ~ ~ ~ ~ ~ ~ ~ ~ ~ ~

were not the kind you keep in your billfold. They were huge — the size a photographer would display in his studio window to advertise his trade. I ignored her unenthusiastic, damp greeting, announced myself to my new boss and, after a brief chat with him, he showed me to my desk and returned to his office.

I slid into my chair, faced the bare, pristine surface of my big new desk and just sat there thinking, what am I supposed to do? Getting a cup of coffee and smiling a lot seemed like the best plan of action.

As I sat there, I thought about JBN's two secretaries, Leslie and Teri. Best friends, they had been there for some time and didn't seem to relish the idea of another person in "their" office. I had the distinct impression they didn't particularly feel the need of someone to manage the place — they were managing just fine, thank you very much!

Teri had been polite and pleasant during the few times we had met, but stayed pretty much to herself on my first day at the office. Leslie, on the other hand, was out to show me who was boss, and it wasn't going to be me. She had a chip on her shoulder from the very first moment I was introduced to her, and and I felt its presence every time we met. She was the one person I needed to get on my side. Even before coming to work I had planned my strategy to win her over — how nice I would be to her, how important I would make her feel — and so on. No Problem!

But the best-laid plans often disintegrate in the blink of an eye. Just around midday I responded to loud hammering coming from the reception area. The new bride was energetically pounding nails in the wall behind her desk in preparation for hanging her wedding pictures. To my suggestion that her choice of art was not appropriate for a law office, she shouted a loud "fuck you" without missing a

~ ~ ~ ~ ~ ~ ~ ~ ~ ~ ~ ~ ~ ~ ~ ~ ~ ~ ~

beat with her hammer.

I quietly told her to pack her things, not to forget her picture gallery, and leave. I could do without that.

Omigod! What had I done? In less than four hours on my new job I had fired the receptionist. What was wrong with me? How would I explain the crisis I had created?

To my great surprise and relief, my dear boss took the news in stride and was rather sanguine about the whole thing. Calmly, he suggested I call in temporary help, and start looking around for someone more suitable. He told me he never liked her very much anyway. I was apprehensive my drastic action would put a strain my new office relationship with Teri.

Well, done is done, and I would cross that bridge when I came to it. In retrospect, firing Ms. Foulmouth was a smart move on my part, because no one else gave me any trouble for a long, long time.

The very next day, I was told to get ready for a client board meeting the following morning. I was to figure out the dilution of the shares of common stock if all the preferred stock was converted, the phantom stock was accounted for and the stock options were exercised. Right! Of course. Why don't I do that? I had half a day to complete a task I didn't understand at all. I had never even seen a stock certificate, let alone figure out what? I wanted to laugh and say, "Could you run that by me again?" But I kept quiet and nodded, "Sure."

I pored through the files, read all the agreements and contracts, and went over the stock book. I plowed my way through the documents as if my life depended on it — in a way it did. After several uninterrupted hours of seeking, searching and going over every minute detail, every scrap of paper, I had the information I needed. There was one hurdle

~ ~ ~ ~ ~ ~ ~ ~ ~ ~ ~ ~ ~ ~ ~ ~ ~ ~ ~ ~

left to jump: convert everything into percentages. I reached for the telephone.

To this day I can hear myself whispering to Gary over the telephone, "To get percentages, do you put the big number into the little number or the little number into the big number?"

With my temples pounding and palms sweating, I put the analysis on the boss's desk. He looked my masterpiece over carefully, made a few editing changes, suggested a different format, and asked me to to make copies for all the board members.

Another first! To this day I have no idea how I did it. This incident taught me a most important lesson: "I can do anything if I try." The secret is to break any project down into doable chunks. I wouldn't do it any differently today. The hardest part is to find a starting place and begin.

Within a few months I was blissfully happy. I loved every minute of every day. I was constantly introduced to something new and different. I met entrepreneurs, other attorneys, accountants, bankers, businessmen, and learned all about raising money to finance new enterprises. These bright people believed that a good portion of Portland's economic future lay in establishing high-tech businesses. And they were right, of course. Today it is a leading business sector in Oregon.

I really didn't understand the concept until I witnessed the parade of budding entrepreneurs marching through our offices who were leaving Tektronix and Hewlett-Packard to build a better mousetrap — mainly their own. They were looking for help in financing their dreams and turned to us to find the necessary funds to build that better mousetrap. My boss was quite instrumental in bringing a good portion of the technology industry to Oregon. It was our firm's

~ ~ ~ ~ ~ ~ ~ ~ ~ ~ ~ ~ ~ ~ ~ ~ ~ ~ ~ ~

Financial Symposium for Emerging Companies in 1982 that helped put our state on the map of the high-tech world.

I was learning new things so fast that I had no time to dwell on the embarrassing fact of how green I had been when I took this job. I went along to every single meeting that involved the firm's activities. I learned firsthand the skills an entrepreneur needed in order to grow an idea into a successful business venture. I learned about banking, accounting and the intricacies of finance.

All of a sudden I was purchasing a computer for our company and using a word processor when I barely knew what it was a short time ago. Everything was new. To this day, I'm amazed I didn't just drop dead from sheer fright. I never dwelled on thoughts like that very long; instead, I tackled the next hurdle, one at a time.

Our accountant taught me the basics of how to keep books and get a trial balance. I learned about blue-sky laws and securities regulations. I learned about some of the games people played in business and how everybody scratched everybody else's back.

I learned the subtle intricacies of negotiating straight from the master. My boss had an uncanny talent of putting people — entrepreneur and venture capitalist — with opposing views in the same room, listen to them talk and argue and gnash around without getting anywhere. After an hour or so, he would calmly suggest something that lowered the opposing parties' defenses and transformed the deal at hand into a winning situation.

I learned that the entrepreneur is in love with his company and doesn't want to give any of it away. On the other hand, the venture capitalist is in love with his money and doesn't want to give it away without getting a good share of the entrepreneur's company.

~ ~

I learned a hard-and-fast rule: You had to give up something in order to get something.

I learned that I did have that rod of steel in my back, was smart, and could learn anything.

In just a few months I had gotten an education that would serve me for the rest of my life. I was filling up compartments of my mind with information like a huge sponge soaking up a major flood. I felt a greater sense of community with the people around me, and I blossomed. It was quite an introduction to self-discovery, personal satis-faction and an affirmation of my unlimited abilities.

My boss had a difficult time tending to business. He was attracted to each new entrepreneur like a moth to the flame and often neglected his other clients. He possessed an extraordinary amount of brains and charm but fell short on follow-through. I worked hard at holding things together to keep his house of cards from tumbling down. I was the buffer between him and our clients, who were clamoring for the completion of their projects. I became the go-between for him and his associates who needed his time, advice and expertise. I was the person between him and our vendors, stalling for time when we didn't collect enough money to pay our bills. On top of that, I acted in his behalf at the bank where we kept borrowing money to keep the company afloat.

I worked long days, and hours into the night. I actually started reading and editing the offering memorandums in an attempt to stay abreast of the work. Gary didn't like it.

One morning, as I was getting ready to leave for work, he faced me, "Why are you willing to work this hard?" he asked in a flat voice and closed face.

"The work has to get done, and I'm enjoying it," I responded, somewhat surprised.

~ ~ ~ ~ ~ ~ ~ ~ ~ ~ ~ ~ ~ ~ ~ ~ ~ ~ ~ ~

"It's a good thing the man isn't a brain surgeon or you'd be doing brain surgery," he yelled back.

I shrugged and turned away. He did have a point. However, I certainly didn't want to be a brain surgeon, but I loved the many-faceted world of business.

June 1980

Dear Mother,

I don't know how to tell you this. I can't quite believe it myself. Remember I mentioned to you on my visit last month that I thought Gary wasn't crazy about me anymore? Well, mother, my heart pounded all the way home, because I was afraid to see him at the airport and face the truth about our marriage. It was as plain as the nose on his face. When I came off the jetway, he was leaning against a post and didn't even look at me. I could hardly walk to the baggage claim and make small talk, because the gulf between us felt wider than the Pacific Ocean. How did he get so far away from me? How can my working make him feel so inadequate that he can't be with me any longer?

What do you think I should do? Quitting my job won't help, because I won't be happy. And if I don't quit, he won't be happy. I desperately want to find common ground with him again. I never wanted to become a divorce statistic. I'm trying to talk him into counseling sessions, but he isn't very interested. He is so angry, and I don't know where all this anger of his is coming from. He's been so quiet all these years. I guess he's been saving up for now!

~ ~ ~ ~ ~ ~ ~ ~ ~ ~ ~ ~ ~ ~ ~ ~ ~ ~ ~

I wish he'd shared his feelings with me along
the way; perhaps I could have made some sense of
it — perhaps? I thought we loved each other.
Now what? Send chicken soup!
Your sad daughter,
Karen
xoxoxo

It was true: just as I was flying high, within six
months, Gary brought me crashing down to earth with the
news that he was leaving me. I was stunned. We had a good
marriage — or did we? What happened?

As it turned out, he was intent on having dinner on the
table at six o'clock sharp without fail. He felt it was not
good for the children to see me "working so hard." These
were feeble excuses for what was really bothering him —
but he wouldn't talk about that.

I pleaded with him to stay, imploring him not to throw
away seventeen years of marriage just because I wanted to
work. Gary was anger personified. He moved into the guest
room while I kept pleading with him for four months to
keep our marriage alive.

A few days before Thanksgiving, angry beyond
reason, he walked out. His parting words were short and
terse: "If you want to live life in the fast lane, you can live
it by yourself."

To say I was devastated doesn't come close to the way
I felt. I forced myself to put one foot in front of the other. I
paced endlessly round and round my dining room table
trying to get a grip on myself, attempting to comprehend the
new twist my life had taken on the road to where? What had
gone wrong? How did this happen? Why couldn't I have

~ ~ ~ ~ ~ ~ ~ ~ ~ ~ ~ ~ ~ ~ ~ ~ ~ ~ ~ ~

stayed put? Was it all me? Was I the only one out of step with the rest of the world?

I mustn't forget I had been warned before. Then, I had fallen back into the fold of Gary's expectations or, should I say, demands. I had complied, acquiesced. I had put his needs before mine. Why did I expect him to act differently? Why couldn't I have my marriage and have me as well?

Now what? I was afraid of facing a future alone and on my own.

The children reacted strongly to the situation. It took Lisa years to get over her parents' divorce. Mark seemed to handle it better, but then maybe boys don't show distress as easily as girls do. I tried to bring sanity and logic into that troubled period in our lives, but Lisa screamed and yelled at me over and over how much she hated me for getting a job which in turn made her father leave home. Divorce is a most traumatic experience for families, and ours was no exception. It was awful.

By the time the new year rolled around, my desolation turned into resolve, and I was determined to make the best of it. If I was going to be alone with the children, I was not going to permit our standard of living to go down. I'd get going and make up for lost time. Besides, I was discovering — reluctantly at that — I enjoyed being by myself: I enjoyed evenings by myself; I enjoyed a new and different freedom I had not experienced before. Being single might not be so bad after all. I approached my fortieth birthday in February eager and unencumbered.

As it turned out, it would be four years before Gary and I said our final goodbye. By that time I was more than ready to fend for myself. My career had taken off, and I was no longer apprehensive about being on my own. I had

~ ~ ~ ~ ~ ~ ~ ~ ~ ~ ~ ~ ~ ~ ~ ~ ~ ~ ~ ~

acquired freedom from fear. I enjoyed taking responsibility for myself.

Even though the end of our marriage feels sad to this day, leaving Gary was necessary for me to be able to follow my own path.

LIFE LESSONS

ONE WOMAN

As I write this chapter, I can see the divorce was a long time coming. When it happened, it came as a shock. I had been living "unconsciously," following my instincts, and I didn't pay any attention to what was happening between Gary and me. For many years I entertained the notion that I brought on the divorce. If I had stayed home none of the upheaval would have happened.

I knew the end of our marriage was inevitable. I felt compelled to express myself in the world aside from my contribution at home. I loved my family and wanted what was best for them, but I needed to save myself. As women, many of us are torn between home and career. Most of us feel the need to express ourselves by following our own bliss, yet we want to take care of our children. The choice is difficult. The road is bumpy and the struggle ongoing.

For the last twenty years women have received the message that "You can have it all." That message has recently been revised: "You can have it all, but not at the same time."

Are you living consciously, or just going through the motions? Where are you in your journey?

~ ~ ~ ~ ~ ~ ~ ~ ~ ~ ~ ~ ~ ~ ~ ~ ~ ~ ~ ~

When I went to work, I had a choice as to whether I was going to work outside the home or not. A family could still live on one income back in 1980. Now, most women don't have the luxury of choosing whether or not to work outside the home. It is an economic necessity.

It is difficult for all of us to fully enjoy our lives because of the rush of everyday living. Most women are bone tired from working two full-time jobs: one outside the home and one inside the home. Women still make less than men, they have less economic power in the community and in the home, and they have primary responsibility for caring for the home and family. I've always said, "The women's movement was just that. The women moved and the men stayed right where they were." And who can blame them?

And, to make matters worse, many women feel a lack of community with other women. For centuries women gathered together to discuss their children, their relationships, and the events of their lives. We have become very isolated from that sense of community which has traditionally given us our sense of connection to others. This creates a problem within the family because we rely on our nuclear families for too much of our support. It places enormous pressure on our relationships, particularly with our partners.

Even though I was honestly relieved to be without the pressure of a marital relationship, I was saddened by the realization it wasn't possible for me to have both career and marriage. And even though I loved my new career, I mourned the loss of my homemaker identity.

Divorce spread through America in the wake of the women's movement. Even though women have made great strides in the labor force, marital status is still the biggest determinant of wealth for women. Divorce is a financial transaction. Yet, most women focus on the emotional

~ ~ ~ ~ ~ ~ ~ ~ ~ ~ ~ ~ ~ ~ ~ ~ ~ ~ ~ ~

aspects and shortchange themselves when it comes to making perhaps the biggest financial decisions of their lives.

If you are potentially facing a divorce:

- Make up your mind to be as single-minded as necessary to negotiate the best settlement you can.
- Understand that the best divorce is one that leaves both partners as intact as possible. Don't try to get even for past transgressions; be as graceful and generous as possible, while taking good care of yourself.
- Read one of the numerous good books about divorce.
- Make copies of all your financial records, including tax returns, investment portfolio statements, retirement accounts, credit card bills, insurance policies, living expenses, and pay stubs.
- Don't assume keeping the house is the best thing for you.
- Make sure you have established your own credit history.
- Don't make impulsive spending or selling decisions.
- Give yourself at least three years to recover.
- Nurture yourself and your children as much as possible.

ONE LIFE

I believe we are put on this earth in this physical body so we can learn more about who we are. We can discover our essence — the part that is eternal. We create our circum-

~ ~ ~ ~ ~ ~ ~ ~ ~ ~ ~ ~ ~ ~ ~ ~ ~ ~ ~ ~

stances so we can learn about ourselves. This learning usually comes about when we take risks and stretch ourselves beyond our self-imposed limits.

When I started looking for a job, I was doing just that: looking for a job. I had no preconceived notions about what the job would be, or how it would fit into my life.

As I went through the process of job seeking, my natural instincts surfaced. All of a sudden I knew I wasn't going to take just any job and become a worker bee. I was reaching for something far beyond me so that I could make up for lost time. I wanted to be where I would have been had I not taken out time for my family. I wanted it all. Of course, I couldn't have it all. I had to trade Gary for me.

⇨ If you could have it all, what would it be?
⇨ Why don't you have what you want?
⇨ What prevents you from taking the risk and meeting the challenge?
⇨ What does your inner voice tell you?
⇨ Remember, you create your reality by every word you speak and every thought you think.

For the next few weeks listen carefully how you talk about yourself to yourself.

Do you support yourself and your ideas, or do you tell yourself you are lacking?

Does your internal dialogue go something like this:

"I'm too fat — I'm too old — I hate my hair — I hate my thighs — My breasts are too small — My breasts are too large — I could never do that — Why did I say that?" On and on it goes. One brutal message after the other. It's no wonder we feel so bad about ourselves.

Every time you say something mean to yourself, visualize a huge, octagonal, bright red stop sign and say "Stop" out loud. Do this every single day until your mind

~ ~ ~ ~ ~ ~ ~ ~ ~ ~ ~ ~ ~ ~ ~ ~ ~ ~ ~ ~

quits telling you what a low-life, undeserving, poor excuse for a woman you are.

On the flip side, start telling yourself every single day — maybe while you're in the shower — how truly special you are, what a wonder you are, that you deserve your heart's desire.

Do this for a month and you will be thrilled how much better you feel.

Notice how much better the people around you feel about you, too.

THE MONEY MYSTIQUE

Don't be afraid to ask for things! How can you get anything unless you ask for it? When I began my job search, I wasn't focused at all. I just wanted a job. I remember thinking, "If Gary isn't going to work, then I am." That was my motivation — simply to get out of the house and find something to do.

But when I got going, I realized that there was more to working than just getting a job. I started to be more selective in looking at an offer. If I was going to put in eight hours a day someplace, I wanted it to be fulfilling. If I was going to invest my life energy, I wanted to be well compensated.

I realize that the reason I wasn't afraid was the fact that I did not need a job for economic reasons. We had enough money coming in to pay the bills. The job was intended to give me a means of self-expression rather than to pay the bills. That alone gave me the confidence to interview without fear or apprehension. Prospective employers can tell if an applicant is desperate and immediately cut an interview short.

~ ~ ~ ~ ~ ~ ~ ~ ~ ~ ~ ~ ~ ~ ~ ~ ~ ~ ~ ~

I learned to focus on the goal of earning $25,000 a year. I have proven time and again to myself that knowing exactly what I want is tantamount to having it.

- ❧ Identify what you want in your career, your relationships, and in your finances.
- ❧ Focus on the single most important aspect in the most microscopic detail you can imagine — both goal and timing.
- ❧ Write it down one hundred times.
- ❧ Carry it with you in your wallet.
- ❧ Read it twice a day.
- ❧ Know you can have it.
- ❧ Once you are comfortable with it, share it with someone you trust.
- ❧ Form a Mastermind group and use the Mastermind.

A Mastermind group is a wonderful resource for helping you identify your heart's desire and focus on how to get what you want. For the past year, I have offered a class called Masterminding Your Money, and miracles happen.

The Mastermind works under the theory that we are more powerful when we focus our energy collectively for each one of us rather than focusing on something by ourselves.

The Mastermind works when:
- ❧ We feel genuine gratitude for the everyday things in our lives.
- ❧ We are single minded in purpose and willing to take action to achieve our goal.
- ❧ We are generous with ourselves and others.
- ❧ We understand the essence of our goal, and we are willing to give up our attachment to the

~ ~ ~ ~ ~ ~ ~ ~ ~ ~ ~ ~ ~ ~ ~ ~ ~ ~ ~ ~

outcome. For example, we might think we want a wood stove, a fireplace, or a new furnace. But what we really want is heat. We need to trust the Universe will provide us with the essence of our desire. The challenge is to recognize it when it appears before us.

- We are committed to making a genuine contribution to others and to the planet.

- We are willing to use our time and resources to achieve our goals. Wishing won't make it so. We have to be willing to put in the time. How we spend our time is very important. Many of us make plans, wish for something, hope for success, yet we don't spend our time making those dreams come true. As the Bible says, "Faith without works is dead." Or, in New Age vernacular, "Head, heart, hands," or, better yet, "Just do it."

~ ~

CHAPTER SIX

~ ~ ~ ~ ~ ~ ~ ~ ~ ~ ~ ~ ~ ~ ~ ~ ~ ~ ~

"Making the decision to have a child — it's momentous.
It is to decide forever to have your heart
go walking around outside your body."
– Elizabeth Stone

Life kept turning out surprises for me. One of them was my divorce from Gary. It took place in January of 1981. We stayed in touch, saw each other frequently, held hands and, surprise — we were remarried in May of 1982.

It may sound strange, but saying goodbye to one's first love and the father of one's children is hard to do. Even though I wanted the divorce by the time it became final, I was not ready to accept the reality of a failed marriage, nor was I willing to admit my mistakes. So, we'd try again. Maybe we could still make it work.

~ ~ ~ ~ ~ ~ ~ ~ ~ ~ ~ ~ ~ ~ ~ ~ ~ ~ ~

How can it work when the same people do the same things (again), have the same ideas (again), expect the same things from each other (again), disappoint each other (again), and experience the same frustrations (again). Nothing had changed.

By then Lisa had graduated from high school and gone off to a small liberal arts college in Tacoma, Washington, not far from home. She had been an honor student and was readily admitted to the school of her choice. We were so proud of her. Lisa's education was particularly important to me because I felt so shortchanged by my own college experience. I was determined she'd go to college. Not unlike other mothers, I realized I wanted to live out my dreams through Lisa. Bright, full of fun and beautiful, Lisa had the world at her feet.

Yet, instinctively, but buried deeply, I knew Lisa was having a hard time. Something was not right with our bright and beautiful daughter. I had ignored all the signs of anorexia since she was thirteen years old, and I continued to look the other way. Except for associating Lisa's incipient condition vaguely to the publicized story of Karen Carpenter, who died of heart failure brought on by anorexia, I ignored my misgivings about my daughter. Ostrich-like, I chose to stick my head in the sand.

All through junior high, Lisa was not just petite, she was tiny. She exercised constantly and ate only oranges. I wasn't worried one bit. If I had heard of anorexia, it had been a fleeting bit of news I may have glimpsed in *People* magazine. Like snowflakes falling on a warm sidewalk, it didn't stick. I hid the magazine from Lisa. I didn't want her to "get any ideas." By ninth grade she was wearing contact lenses, was five-foot-seven inches tall, beautifully proportioned, and quite lovely. My hidden fears about having a

~ ~ ~ ~ ~ ~ ~ ~ ~ ~ ~ ~ ~ ~ ~ ~ ~ ~ ~ ~

child with an eating disorder abated. I believed she had made it through the difficult, vulnerable junior high school years, and all was well.

Lisa was popular in school — busy, active, smart and seemingly happy. So much for the surface. Underneath, she harbored a seething, self-feeding caldron of destructive thought patterns. She believed life would be perfect if she were thin enough — thinner. During her senior year we had a lot of differences and didn't get along very well. Again, I chalked it up to "normal" mother-daughter-teenage behavior.

She completed her first quarter at college and came home for a visit immediately after registering for winter semester and dropped her bombshell on us. She led Gary and me into her bedroom, sat us down and calmly explained to us that she had an eating disorder and wouldn't be able to return to school. She needed treatment.

The deep suspicions I'd harbored, along with murky chunks of guilt, surfaced and I had to face my own failure to act earlier to help my daughter. I took refuge in the fact that now that Lisa's condition was out in the open; perhaps together we could find ways to heal and recover.

True to character, Gary said little. Consequently, we rarely discussed Lisa's illness, nor did we speak about our problems. I was devastated. I could berate myself about all the things I could have/should have seen, heard and done, but it wouldn't change the fact that my daughter was ill — desperately ill.

Gary took Lisa back to school to pack her things and return home. College would have to wait. Lisa had put her life on hold. I wanted to talk to someone — someone safe, someone who knew me and loved me. I asked my sister Anne to meet me for lunch at Piccolo Mondo, our favorite

~ ~ ~ ~ ~ ~ ~ ~ ~ ~ ~ ~ ~ ~ ~ ~ ~ ~ ~ ~

restaurant. We chatted about a hundred things as if there was nothing wrong in my life. I kept rearranging pieces of my salad on the plate, while trying not to choke on a mouthful of greens. It wasn't going to be easy. But when you're really close to a person, you just can't talk "around" things, masking subterfuges and skirting the real issues.

Finally, I blurted it all out. "This isn't just to talk about Lisa's eating disorder. It's about my marriage. It's about me. It's about Gary and me. I feel as if I've jumped off a cliff and I'm still falling. I don't know if it will end. How far down is down? Will I survive it? Will Lisa? Will any of us?"

I put down my fork and looked at Anne expectantly, as if she held the answers to my puzzles. Or did I already have the answers but refused to listen?

Anne stared at me in disbelief. We had been through so much together and shared each other's problems and joys. Anne has four children — two are the same ages as mine, and they went through school together. We shared our lives, our children — from picnics and holidays to skiing Mount Hood. This wasn't just my family tragedy; it was hers as well.

We talked about the devastating effects of anorexia. Then Anne questioned me about Gary. My answers revealed the truth about our marriage.

"Gary and I are too different," I replied without hesitation. "We don't respond to crisis the same way. Me being me," I continued, "I probably overreact. Gary being Gary, he underplays the danger Lisa is in. Our bond may not be strong enough to withstand this tug-of-war. My life as I've known it is over — out the window, gone."

Anne reached over and laid her hand reassuringly on mine. There wasn't much more to say. She knew me as well as I knew myself. Our hearts and thoughts came from the

~ ~ ~ ~ ~ ~ ~ ~ ~ ~ ~ ~ ~ ~ ~ ~ ~ ~ ~ ~

same source. We understood each other only too well.

When we got up to leave, Anne hugged me for the longest time, kissed me on the cheek and promised to be there for me. I knew I could count on her. I drove myself back to work, sad and aware that I was entering a black fog so dense I might not find my way out.

Then there was the shame. My whole body ached with shame as I silently recited a litany of my "shameful" doings that threatened to scar my heart and soul forever. Shame and guilt. Shame for not being a better mother, for putting my need to work before her needs. I blamed myself for every single unthoughtful deed and action I had performed since Lisa came into the world eighteen years before. I blamed myself for all the hurts and wrongs she may have suffered. I discovered later that it would be weeks before I could confide my misery to close friends, and years before I could talk about it without being overwhelmed by punishing feelings of guilt and shame. I felt utterly alone.

The nightmares brought on by Lisa's eating disorder became an all-consuming part of my life. I no longer could pretend that things were right, when they weren't. I had to live in the truth regardless of the pain. Pretending "things" don't exist does not make them go away. Life teaches lessons that have to be learned, and the earlier the better. The cost of learning life's lessons is high, and I had to pay up.

The next few months were a special kind of hell I couldn't have dreamed up in my wildest imagination. Lisa interviewed one doctor after another, looking for someone she felt could help her. I continued to work and found a welcome relief in the daily business activities that made such different demands on me. Lisa went to the hospital for intensive treatment. The months went by and the whole

~ ~ ~ ~ ~ ~ ~ ~ ~ ~ ~ ~ ~ ~ ~ ~ ~ ~ ~ ~

family underwent therapy. Mark, the easy-going, balanced one, balked; Gary minimized the situation; Lisa was stoic, and I played my emotions to the hilt. I was used to uproar and drama, and this family crisis was the perfect stage setting.

I fumed and fussed, I pleaded and cajoled with Lisa, trying to talk her out of anorexia and into health and normality. I tried to problem-solve with Gary, who wanted no part of it. I would have to hit him over the head with a two-by-four just to get him to admit that we indeed had serious problems.

After a few months of trying to direct our family play into a happy ending, I began seeing a therapist. I spoke with her as often as three times a week, just to get through the next day. It was touch and go with Lisa. Would she survive?

The doctor didn't help when she offered her professional opinion and gloomy statistics. She said," You need to know that, on a scale of one to a hundred, Lisa is a hundred. Ten to fifteen percent of anorexia patients die. Take a good look at the odds and prepare yourself."

Harsher words were never spoken. I looked in vain for the tiniest sliver of comfort as I ran her appraisal of Lisa's more-than-shaky future over and over in my mind. But both the doctor and I had overlooked something of the greatest importance. We had not counted on Lisa's fierce spirit.

Looking back, I truly believe that this was the most difficult time of my life. I was experiencing an intense, screaming kind of pain that left my spirit more dead than alive most days. Nothing could get in or out of my consciousness without passing through my pain first. I felt as if every thought in my head, my feelings and my emotions were wrapped in a transparent layer of onionskin through which everything filtered into and out of my very

~ ~ ~ ~ ~ ~ ~ ~ ~ ~ ~ ~ ~ ~ ~ ~ ~ ~ ~ ~

being. Everything was touched and tainted by my pain.

Outrage and disappointment were my steady companions. I felt so guilty. I felt so responsible. Why hadn't I been able to protect my child? What had happened to make my beautiful Lisa deliberately starve herself? What kind of a society was it which encouraged women to be thin and unhealthy? And anorexia was a disease nobody talked about.

I remember one incident with blinding clarity, and when I recall it I still experience the same mute shock as I did when it happened. I was on my way to town and had stopped at a gas station. While the attendant filled my tank, I was looking straight ahead through the windshield, when I saw an emaciated skeleton in baggy pants walking down the sidewalk in my direction. My thoughts immediately turned to Lisa, when suddenly I realized that this pitiful being of skin and bones was Lisa. *This was my child.*

Every drop of blood seemed to drain from my heart at that moment and yet, I was able to roll down the car window, lean out casually and call to her. She smiled when she saw me, and said, "Hi! What are you doing here?"

"I'm on my way back to the office after a meeting. How are you, darling?"

On and on went the small talk until she bent down, gave me an obligatory peck on the cheek and went on her way with her pants flapping against her bone-thin legs like a tired sail in the wind. I thought I would die. But, of course, I didn't. Human nature has a magical, built-in, deep-seated survival system that takes over, sets you on your heels, turns you around, and lets you start all over again. It worked for me.

But I also believe my job saved my life. At work I felt sane, rational and in control. No matter how complicated

~ ~ ~ ~ ~ ~ ~ ~ ~ ~ ~ ~ ~ ~ ~ ~ ~ ~ ~ ~

life could be, there was an accountable order in the business environment, and cause and effect were reliable and predictable quantities. I poured myself into my tasks. I was responsible for my activities and was able to handle them all. Waves of pain continued to wash over me much like the tides. But I didn't drown. I realized that I had to let Lisa go. Let her own her eating disorder and take responsibility for her condition — for her life. All I could give to her was my love, and perhaps the unwavering belief that she could make it on her own.

Gradually, I came to realize that I had not made her sick.

The illness was Lisa's expression, her way of reacting to life, and I didn't cause any of it. I became aware that if I could make her sick, I could make her well. When the veil of my confusion was lifted with sanity and reason, I could see reality. I sure as hell couldn't make Lisa well; therefore, I couldn't have made her sick.

During her first week in the hospital, Gary and I joined our daughter in group family therapy sessions. There we all sat, the bright, affluent parents of bright and obsessed young women. We introduced ourselves to each other, in the presence of the invisible guests — shame, guilt, anger and despair.

We made brittle talk about our responses to our daughters' eating disorders. I listened with half a brain, silently screaming for somebody, anybody, to let me out of there. An older woman's voice reached me. She smiled at her daughter and said, "My daughter has battled anorexia since she was fifteen years old. She's thirty-five now. We started coming to these meetings twenty years ago, and they have really helped me deal with her issues."

I listened in horrified silence. My inner voice

~ ~ ~ ~ ~ ~ ~ ~ ~ ~ ~ ~ ~ ~ ~ ~ ~ ~ ~ ~

screamed ruthlessly, "No, No, No! This isn't your illness. This is Lisa's illness. You can't take it on for her. You're not going to be sitting in this chair twenty years from now telling the same story."

After the meeting, I calmly informed Lisa and Gary of the decision I had reached. "I'm sorry, but I'm not that kind of a mother. I'm not coming back. I'm going to let this eating disorder be Lisa's issue, not mine. I'll go to family therapy but, by and large, I'm not owning this — you are, Lisa."

My heart was barely beating when I let myself out of the psychiatric unit at St. Vincent's Hospital that night. In uneasy silence, Gary and I drove home. Not a word passed between us. Perhaps we were both horrified by my bottom-line attitude.

Letting my child own her illness freed me up somewhat to live my own life. As I emerged, purpose and reason emerged again and, in spite of the pain, I knew I would be stronger. I continued therapy and explored every corner of my relationship with Gary. As the months dragged by, I gradually realized that being married to Gary for the second time was not going to work for me. Every time I stood my ground about Lisa, he would say something damaging like, "If she doesn't survive, it will be your fault." Or, "I don't know why you are so worried. She's fine."

We were coming at each other from opposite corners, bearing contradictory views and clashing life principles.

By the end of that long, unhappy summer, Mark and Lisa not only noticed the widening rift in their parents' relationship, but they even suggested we bring it to an end. The Friday night before Labor Day 1984, I walked into the house from a City Club meeting and faced Gary at the dining room table. Without any forethought, I blurted out,"

~ ~ ~ ~ ~ ~ ~ ~ ~ ~ ~ ~ ~ ~ ~ ~ ~ ~ ~ ~

You have to leave, you know."

With a brief nod of his head, Gary conveyed his silent agreement, and we spent the next few hours discussing the details of our separation. This time for good.

September 1984

Dear Gloria,

Gary and I are getting divorced again. I know it sounds crazy, but we can't make it together anymore. The kids are feeling all right about it, but still, it's really hard. The best part is knowing it has to be. The last time we separated I had so many doubts, but I don't have any now. Even though he is the nicest person in the world, he can't really be himself when he is with me. I am just too strong for him to maintain his sense of self.

The worst part is that we will never walk down the aisle together at our children's weddings; we will never enjoy our grandchildren together, and we will never be able to share our history with anyone. That just kills me.

I wonder if we would have made it if Lisa hadn't gotten sick. We are so different in our responses that there is no way we could make it through this experience intact. Gary pretends it isn't a big deal, and I feel it's the worst thing that ever happened. So you see, we can't possibly get through it unscathed. Probably we should have stayed divorced, but having the family together was so important. It still is. I try to believe we are still a family. The form is just different.

You always tell me I have the worst things happen to me and the best. I'd be happy to get off

~ ~ ~ ~ ~ ~ ~ ~ ~ ~ ~ ~ ~ ~ ~ ~ ~ ~ ~

this roller coaster I call my life and find some peace
of mind. I wonder if and when that day will ever be.
Thank you for your love and your support. Where
would I be without you?

I'll call you soon.

Karen

xoxoxo

Through all the uproar, the uncertainties and pain,
Mark remained steadfast. He never wavered once and
brought his gift of equanimity, at least to me. He continued
to go to school, played baseball, made good grades, went to
the prom, and was an all-around joy. Even though he didn't
like going to therapy, he went along with the program. He
mentioned one time that "It's hard being the only sane
person in the family." His cheerful and disarming ways
helped all of us keep some sort of balance in our daily lives.
He was fearless about taking things apart and equally brave
putting them back together — and that included reducing
his second car to a large assortment of parts, nuts and bolts,
and unerringly rebuilding the automobile.

He never was a problem. When he was in junior high
school, he decided to peroxide his bangs. I thought it looked
terrible, but I didn't comment on it. I told a friend, "If
bleaching his bangs is the extent of his teenage rebellion,
I'm the luckiest mother in the world." I never had to worry
about him.

The caring and understanding ways of my friends and
family still amaze me, and they truly were, and continue to
be, that proverbial "wind beneath my wings." Slowly, I
picked myself up, re-thought and re-directed my life,
adjusting, with Gary gone, to the three of us as the family.

~ ~ ~ ~ ~ ~ ~ ~ ~ ~ ~ ~ ~ ~ ~ ~ ~ ~ ~ ~

As the Fifth Dimension used to sing, there was "One less bell to answer, one less egg to fry."

The demands my job made on me were a welcome relief from living with someone who had an eating disorder. What I could handle in business, with organization and logic, didn't apply at home. Life with Lisa was difficult, to say the least. But without Gary's presence, I could at least face the situation head-on.

My therapist, in tandem with Lisa's counselor, helped me to understand the guidelines I had to follow dealing with my daughter. The most important one was that Lisa had to keep her weight at 115 pounds, or she had to move out of the house. That was the boundary we set. Anorexics are skilled manipulators and can be rational in every other aspect except where their bodies are concerned. It was crucial to Lisa's survival that I not let her manipulate me. It was not an easy task.

I will never forget the night of Halloween 1984. Lisa, who had a good job with a prestigious law firm, had been taken to the hospital that morning for IV therapy. She not only didn't eat, she didn't drink fluids either. She explained in stubborn defense of her action that she wasn't thirsty, or hungry, for that matter, and even drinking water made her feel fat.

One of her friends called to inform me that Lisa was in the hospital, and was so dehydrated that the nurse couldn't find a vein to administer the IV. I knew this would be the end for me.

My heart filled with agony; I called my therapist, asking her what I should do. After she conferred with my daughter's counselor, she called me back and advised me firmly that I had to make good on my threat and make Lisa leave the house, "It may break your heart to do so, but if you

~ ~ ~ ~ ~ ~ ~ ~ ~ ~ ~ ~ ~ ~ ~ ~ ~ ~ ~ ~

don't set limits," my therapist said, "Lisa will not survive."

I remember my voice reached an almost hysterical pitch when I screamed my pain into the telephone receiver in protest. "What will she do? Where will she go? How can I do this terrible thing? She is so sick! She's my little girl," I sobbed, hopelessly enmeshed in the web of tragedy Lisa had spun for all of us.

The calm voice of my therapist persisted: "Taking care of yourself is the only hope Lisa has of taking care of herself. You must let her go. You must make her leave." I carefully replaced the receiver in its cradle, put my head down, and cried and cried until there were no tears left in my reservoir of sorrow.

Back home I waited for Lisa to come through the door. I was shaking from head to toe. Closing my eyes brought no relief, because the awful scenes I made in my mind of Lisa failing on her own struck me like a knife in my heart. I was grateful for Mark's absence. He was out having his Halloween fun.

Eventually, Lisa breezed in as if nothing had happened — as though everything was perfectly normal — just another day at work.

Looking into her eyes, I gathered the remains of my courage and steeled myself for what was to come. "Do you weigh 115 pounds?"

"No," she replied in a small voice.

I wanted to gather her in my arms and hold her safe forever. Instead I looked straight into her thin, lovely face and said in a quiet voice, "Well, you must leave. I warned you. I'll give you 24 hours."

Of course, Lisa protested and we argued, even as my heart was breaking, but I held my ground.

I knew the only way for Lisa to become whole, the

~ ~ ~ ~ ~ ~ ~ ~ ~ ~ ~ ~ ~ ~ ~ ~ ~ ~ ~

only road to her healing, was for her to choose between life and death — on her own. No longer could I permit her to shift the burden of her reality to me. She had to shoulder her own inadequacy and face down her destructive feelings. She had to save herself or let go forever. That night with Lisa was the worst of my life. To this day, I do not like Halloween.

Lisa left the next day carrying my heart with her.

Mark had not been at home during my battle with his sister. When he returned, I told him what happened, and in a feeble attempt to make light of it, I said, "First your dad, then Lisa! You'd better be careful or you're next." We just looked at each other and said no more.

Mark was a senior that year and soon would go his own way. We had a wonderful time, just the two of us. I didn't need him to be the man of the house; I just needed him there to keep me grounded because I felt like a crazy person.

And Lisa, who is the hero of this story, fought like a wildcat to stay alive. It was touch and go for years, but she never gave up on herself. Her will to live, her indomitable spirit to win, is remarkable. With the demons banished, she now has created a wonderful life for herself. She has my absolute admiration and respect. She has been the greatest teacher for me, and her story has touched so many. Perhaps one day she will share her passages in her own book.

~ ~ ~ ~ ~ ~ ~ ~ ~ ~ ~ ~ ~ ~ ~ ~ ~ ~ ~

LIFE LESSONS

ONE WOMAN

Separating myself from my child was nearly impossible for me. Lisa's pain was my pain. I identified with her heart and soul. I lived with the illusion that I could control another person. I believed that if I wanted something for another person and wanted it badly enough, I could force that person to do my will.

Lisa taught me one of life's greatest lessons. We are responsible for ourselves and nobody else. Even now I have a hard time understanding that I can change only myself. It's so much easier to focus outside. "If only he/she would change, I could be happy." It never works.

Just for today:

- Look at your relationships. Are they outer-focused or inner-focused?
- Does somebody else's opinion of you matter more than your opinion of yourself?
- What happens if you focus only on your behavior in a difficult situation?
- How does it feel to be responsible for your own feelings and the state of your own mind?

ONE LIFE

In spite of Lisa's illness and her close brush with disaster, I knew I had to save myself. Lisa and I went through years of conflict. From time to time she refused to see me, admonishing, "Your intolerance of my eating disorder makes it impossible for me to talk to you. I am my eating disorder."

~ ~ ~ ~ ~ ~ ~ ~ ~ ~ ~ ~ ~ ~ ~ ~ ~ ~ ~ ~

I replied. "To me you are my beautiful, courageous daughter — not an eating disorder. I refuse to respond to you in that way. I want you to know I love you and support the healthy part of you. I'll be here when you call."

Several of my women clients come to me pretty well spent — emotionally and financially. Most of them are not well off financially. Several of these women have enjoyed prosperity in the past. To my question of what happened to their money, they invariably reply, "I don't know. I guess I gave it away."

I advise them to take care of themselves first. I use the following as an example:

When you are on an airplane and the flight attendant describes measures to be taken in the event of an emergency, what is the most pertinent instruction she gives to passengers? It goes like this: "If you're traveling with small children or someone who needs your help, when the oxygen mask drops down, put your mask on first."

"Put your mask on first." In other words, you must take care of yourself before you can take care of others.

The most important role I see for women is to model responsible, adult behavior for their children and friends. Life deals all of us a rotten hand from time to time. It's not the cards so much as the way we play them. We need to develop mastery over life and demonstrate our competency, particularly to our children. We are all teachers. We can teach others that we are strong and capable. Act as if you are strong and you will grow strong. It is even better if you can enjoy yourself in the process.

When we take on responsibility for others, we are essentially telling them that we know what is better for them than they do. We convey the subliminal message, "You don't know how to take care of yourself. I know you

~ ~ ~ ~ ~ ~ ~ ~ ~ ~ ~ ~ ~ ~ ~ ~ ~ ~ ~ ~

will fail without me." This creates dependency and weakness.

It is much more helpful and inspiring if we can say to others, "I have confidence in your willingness and ability to manage your life in a healthy way. I know you don't need me to tell you what to do. I am here to love and support you."

- ☙ Look around you to see who you are trying to control and who is trying to control you.
- ☙ Is this comfortable for you?
- ☙ Are you modeling competency for others?
- ☙ When you meditate, visualize yourself as a competent, powerful person. What does it feel like to be competent and powerful?
- ☙ What prevents you from feeling powerful in your life, work, or relationships?
- ☙ How are you causing this to happen? How can you change it?

THE MONEY MYSTIQUE

Lisa's hospital stays and her therapy over the years have cost hundreds of thousands of dollars. Only $6,500 of the costs were covered by insurance. Fortunately, in the beginning Gary and I had the money available to help her. After several years we were tapped out, and we suggested Lisa finance her illness on her own.

She worked and went to school, unless she was hospitalized. Interestingly enough, she got financial support from the hospital to stay in the program. She did an excellent job managing her hospitalizations and, subsequently, her outpatient therapy.

~ ~ ~ ~ ~ ~ ~ ~ ~ ~ ~ ~ ~ ~ ~ ~ ~ ~ ~ ~

I believe that allowing her the privilege of managing her illness emotionally, physically and financially led her back to health.

- What financial matters are you managing for others that they would be better left to manage themselves?
- How much time and emotional energy do you give to others?
- Do you attempt to make others happy by giving them money?
- Do you believe people love you more because you take care of them even when they are old enough to take care of themselves?
- How well do you take care of yourself in times of crisis?
- Do you have enough insurance to take care of a catastrophic event in your life?

CHAPTER SEVEN

~ ~ ~ ~ ~ ~ ~ ~ ~ ~ ~ ~ ~ ~ ~ ~ ~ ~ ~ ~

"No trumpets sound when the important decisions of our life are made. Destiny is made known silently."
– Agnes de Mille

Balancing the turmoil in my personal life by the positive challenges of the business world was the benefit I sought when I first decided to go to work. I was lucky to have landed a job that offered me an insight into the legal aspects of financing businesses and the intricacies of negotiating. My boss was a master negotiator. My job also brought me into contact with a variety of professionals, all of whom played an active and important role in funding new enterprises or backing the expansion of established companies.

Even though I caught on quickly to the demands of

~ ~ ~ ~ ~ ~ ~ ~ ~ ~ ~ ~ ~ ~ ~ ~ ~ ~ ~

my job, I also realized how ill-prepared I was for the business world. I needed to learn a lot more if I planned to land bigger and more challenging jobs. I wanted to learn about accounting. I understood the necessity of the bottom line to business, and accounting is the key.

Naturally, I decided to get a job with an accounting firm. And if I was going to work in that industry, I might as well link up with one of the big eight international firms, where I could really learn the tricks of the trade. I wanted a job with Touche Ross (now Deloitte & Touche).

My timing was perfect because JBN was giving up his law practice in order to devote his time to being a full-fledged venture capitalist. He wanted to be one of the big boys who located the money to finance new businesses. Our parting was amicable. We wished each other well and moved on. On our last day together he gave me a desk plaque inscribed with the words: "Wonder Woman Works Here."

Pointing to the shiny surface of the brass plaque with its big message, he smiled and said the nicest thing. "This is you. I've never met anyone like you, and it's not likely I ever will again. You've helped me in ways I don't fully understand. Thanks."

Those words came straight from his heart and made me feel good. I reached over and gave him a big hug, and we promised to keep in touch. Of course, we didn't stay in touch, but it was nice to think we would.

I had managed a variety of events for the high-tech industry and was somewhat visible as a player in my own right. I approached a friend of mine at Touche Ross with whom I had worked on several projects and asked him to hire me to do marketing for his firm. Just like that — no need to beat around the bush.

~ ~ ~ ~ ~ ~ ~ ~ ~ ~ ~ ~ ~ ~ ~ ~ ~ ~ ~ ~

My friend told me that one or two of the Touche Ross branches on the East Coast employed marketing people. He offered to check it out with the new partner in charge of the Portland office, and go from there. He called back the next day. "He's interested. Can we meet for lunch tomorrow?"

I was excited. I just knew it would work for one reason — I needed a job. I'll never forget walking into the beautiful gray-and-maroon offices of this prestigious accounting firm on the fourteenth floor of Benjamin Franklin Plaza. Full of confidence, I stepped up to the receptionist, gave her my card and asked to see my friend. Accompanied by the branch's partner and a stunning redhead, who turned out to be the right hand of the man in charge, my friend greeted me warmly.

We settled in for lunch and talked about Touche Ross — what else? I started out by saying, "Your firm has the best people, yet your company seems to be a well-kept secret. I really want to help you land more business." With that, I laid out several marketing ideas and concepts that I had developed for this first meeting. I had an attentive audience who listened carefully and asked a lot of questions. When we parted after the long lunch, I felt as though I'd known these people all my life. Elaine, the beautiful redhead, is still one of my best friends.

My timing must have been perfect. I was offered a job within the week and started working for Touche Ross a short while later.

Sometimes the magic works! I was in heaven. This was the best! The people around me were smart and friendly and a hard-working bunch. I was left on my own to set up a new marketing department, and my endeavors had the managing partner's support. Several of the older partners had a hard time relating to me, and the newly established

~ ~ ~ ~ ~ ~ ~ ~ ~ ~ ~ ~ ~ ~ ~ ~ ~ ~ ~ ~

marketing department. They couldn't understand why the firm needed such an addition and considered me unnecessary overhead.

Our efforts paid off, and and business poured in at a steady rate. It was great and truly satisfying. On top of that, I met some of my closest friends during my time with Touche Ross. Sylvia, with whom I worked, used to tell people, "Karen is a master at dealing with our partners. She can get them to agree to anything with her charm and determination. She never takes no for an answer. To Karen, 'No' merely means, 'Not right now.'"

The one fly in the ointment was the hellacious drinking pattern of the partner-in-charge. It didn't take long for me to realize that this nice man had a serious problem. Booze was the uninvited guest in the offices of our company. His hands started to shake in the morning and were calmed with several martinis over lunch. By about four o'clock in the afternoon, the martinis had worn off, and he rounded us up and hauled us off to the lobby bar at the Marriott Hotel across the street.

I never drank so much in my life. Luckily, alcohol was never a problem for me. It was fun to be on the inside and I didn't think about it too much. From time to time Elaine and I would tell ourselves to cut back on the daily routine of afternoon cocktails, but four o'clock would roll around, and we'd be bellying up to the bar at the Marriott with our boss in the lead.

In spite of everything, business continued to be good. That man may have been an alcoholic, but he knew what he wanted for the firm, and besides, everybody covered for him. I was not aware that some of the partners were not sympathetic about the situation and were about to take matters into their own hands. They fussed and fumed and

~ ~ ~ ~ ~ ~ ~ ~ ~ ~ ~ ~ ~ ~ ~ ~ ~ ~ ~

started to revolt.

The end came for my boss at Touche Ross the same week I decided to divorce Gary in September of 1984. I was in San Francisco for a meeting. My mind was on Gary, knowing he was moving out of our home while I was gone. I received a phone call from Nancy, my secretary, who told me that everything was falling apart at the office. The boss was gone. Nobody was in charge, and I had better get back. There was to be a meeting the following day.

I couldn't believe my ears! I needed this like a pig needs a bicycle.

Before I even returned home, it was quite clear to me that I would need a new job. My instincts told me it would take a few years before the company would run well again. If they didn't know who was in charge of the office, I was in trouble. I knew that the marketing department would be the first to go during a business crisis. Besides, most of my support had come from my boss, and without him I was easy prey.

Everybody in the office was in shock and disbelief. The partners were scrambling for footing. It took months before a new manager was named, and by then it became rather obvious that marketing was no longer going to be a priority. Even though I loved my work, I reluctantly admitted it was time to move on.

By then I had made some interesting discoveries about myself, one of which was that money management appealed to me. I wanted to find out just how money managers made investment decisions for their clients, and how the stock market works. What was this business of investing all about? It was a question I was eager to solve. I set my cap for getting a job in the money management industry. It wasn't hard. I suppose the fact that once you know what you

~ ~ ~ ~ ~ ~ ~ ~ ~ ~ ~ ~ ~ ~ ~ ~ ~ ~ ~ ~

want and stay focused, everything is possible.

I'd rarely let grass grow under my feet and was always on the lookout for the next opportunity. I had made friends with a very nice man who was in the money management business. I wasn't sure just what money management was, but I was going to find out all about it. I met him for lunch and we talked about a brochure he was in the process of completing and about his marketing efforts in general. I had my first introduction to investment policies and money management.

The next time we met, I knew I wanted him to hire me. During lunch I admired his successful and debonnaire demeanor while I kept bombarding him with questions about his company, Capital Trust. He said they had been part of another company and were going out on their own.

Again I felt that rush, that knowing when timing is perfect. After lunch, I casually suggested he needed a full-time marketing person. I quietly outlined precisely what such a person could do. In other words, what I could do.

He quickly replied, "I've been thinking the same thing myself. Why don't you come to the office tomorrow morning and meet Ralph, my partner?"

It felt great to know I could make things happen!

The next day, I dressed carefully in a navy silk suit. By that time I was wearing my jewelry again. Maybe wearing lots of glitter didn't work for some, but it sure worked for me. I was just about to leave for the meeting when my phone rang.

It was Lisa. I could hardly tell at first, because her voice was so small and faint.

Barely audible, she said, "I need to go back to the hospital. I'm really sick. I don't know what to do. This morning someone asked me for my phone number and I

~ ~ ~ ~ ~ ~ ~ ~ ~ ~ ~ ~ ~ ~ ~ ~ ~ ~ ~ ~

couldn't remember it. I'm really scared." Her voice trailed off and I told her to stay where she was; I'd be on my way. I quickly called Capital Trust and, without difficulty, changed my appointment to later in the day.

I literally flew out of the office to get to Portland State University, where I picked up my daughter. We stopped briefly at her father's place, where she was staying, and gathered up a few of her belongings in a hurry. Lisa was quiet, not saying a word; she just looked out the window all the way to the hospital. Despair and fear grabbed at my heart as I watched the huge double doors at the hospital entrance swallow her slight form — no bigger than a shadow. Forlornly, she clutched a well-loved teddy bear in one hand, and a backpack in the other. That vision haunts me to this day.

I sat frozen behind the wheel of my car, until someone honked behind me, motioning me to move on. I put the car in gear and slowly left the hospital grounds. I had done this before — but how would it end? Or would it?

As they say at home, I girded up my loins, repaired my makeup, pasted a smile on my face, and drove myself to my interview. The man behind the desk who greeted me was about my age, handsome and bright. I knew it would be fun working for this company. Ralph inquired about my work experience, chatted about his business and a few generalities. He was easy to talk to, and we got along great. Curiosity must have gotten the best of him, because he looked me straight in the face and said, "Tell me about your personal life."

I knew this line of questioning was against the law. I glared at him and replied, "I'm a widow with eight children." He visibly blanched, and managed a weak, "Really?" Instead of an explanation, I laughed uproariously.

~ ~ ~ ~ ~ ~ ~ ~ ~ ~ ~ ~ ~ ~ ~ ~ ~ ~ ~

He joined in my merriment and the deal was done.

True to form, I knew nothing about the industry —
after all, that's why I was there; I wanted to learn. Nor was
I sure what my job was all about. I studied day and night. I
read and re-read quarterly reports, annual reports,
marketing materials, stock market reports and reams of
financial analysis, none of which made any sense. It was
rather distressing. I knew I could catch on, but it was going
to be a slow and tedious process.

In the meantime I discovered to my great satisfaction
that I could really sell, even if I didn't understand what I
was selling. I concluded that human beings buy from other
human beings, and trust is the basis for any transaction. I
didn't need to know everything, I just needed to be honest.
If I couldn't come up with an answer for a prospective
client, I would simply say, "That's a good question. Let me
get back to you." And I did. I never pretended I knew
something I didn't. Besides, it gave me an excuse to call
back. But most importantly, it was the way I learned the
business. Every question was a valid one, and every answer
got filed away in my head.

Just at that time 401(k) plans were coming into their
own. Company after company was thinking about offering
this particular type of retirement plan to its employees. My
job was to sell the plan sponsors on the idea of using Capital
Trust to manage the money in their plan. It was so simple. I
loved my work and appreciated the fact that I was learning
more than what I had set out to do. On one hand I was
learning about the markets and how to put money away for
retirement. On the other hand, I was discovering so many
different kinds of businesses and how they operated. I
received an on-the-job education, a real hands-on program.
And I took advantage of it.

~ ~ ~ ~ ~ ~ ~ ~ ~ ~ ~ ~ ~ ~ ~ ~ ~ ~ ~ ~

In May of 1983, a year after Gary and I married for the second time, a somewhat startling event occurred in my life.

I met a tall, handsome man on a flight to New York. Like any "seasoned" businesswoman, I had a lap full of official-looking papers and was studying my notes for an upcoming meeting in the Big Apple. Chicago passengers boarded our flight, and the man took his seat next to me. He interrupted my train of thought with, "Excuse me, do you have seat number 23E?

Annoyed at the interruption, I answered with a brusque, "Yes," followed by an equally terse, "Why?" I wasn't even looking at him.

"Because I have seat number 23D, and they never put me next to a beautiful woman like you." Well, that was Steve!

He certainly got my attention. I tried to ignore him, but he would have none of it. Conversation developed; he talked, I talked, and by the time we landed in New York, he had given me his mother's telephone number with instructions to call him if I wanted some company in the city, see a play, have dinner. I would be in New York over the weekend and had nothing to do. It sounded innocent enough. As it turned out, he too lived in Portland, had been in Chicago on business, and was on his way to New York to visit his family and celebrate his father's birthday. He was born in the City.

I had no intention of calling him, but the next morning, looking out of my hotel window, I felt differently. I surveyed the crowded streets and the busy traffic below. I saw the tall buildings with their glass and steel and concrete facades reaching for the sky, and I felt small and intimidated facing New York City by myself. I called Steve. He immediately suggested we meet at four o'clock at my hotel and

~ ~ ~ ~ ~ ~ ~ ~ ~ ~ ~ ~ ~ ~ ~ ~ ~ ~ ~

take it from there. I thought nothing of it.

In spite of being a bit overwhelmed by the city, I had to get out and do some exploring on my own. I walked around Manhattan all day, and I fell in love. New York City, the heartbeat of our nation, where everything was happening — business, theatre, entertainment, *The New York Times,* Rizolli's, the Carnegie Deli, the Metropolitan Museum, Central Park. There was no end to this city, and I wanted to see it all. It was grand.

I kept on walking and gawking and, of course, I got lost and would be late for my appointment with Steve. By this time I was mad at myself for having called him in the first place. I had a perfectly good time by myself. I asked for directions that would lead me back to my hotel at 42nd Street and Lexington Avenue. I had no idea where I was. Finally I made it to Donald Trump's grand masterpiece several minutes after four o'clock.

Out of breath, I ran up the stairs of the Grand Hyatt Hotel, ignoring the escalator. I thought I could get by Steve in case he was waiting for me. I wanted to change my clothes for the evening. My head was down and I was within sight of the elevators when I crashed headlong into my new friend just as he was walking towards me.

As I untangled myself from him, I was struck by how good looking he was — with a smile that could melt an avalanche. All I could think was, "Oh no, this man is going to be trouble." I excused myself and raced up to my room, my thoughts and emotions in upheaval. He really was tall, dark and handsome. Heaven help me!

I was married. I didn't "date." What was I feeling? I hadn't noticed anything out of the ordinary on the airplane, or when we walked out of La Guardia together. He certainly was attractive. I admonished myself and listened to my

~ ~ ~ ~ ~ ~ ~ ~ ~ ~ ~ ~ ~ ~ ~ ~ ~ ~ ~ ~

mind chatter. "Just like you, Karen. Make a mountain out of a molehill. Get a grip. Besides, he's probably a lot younger than you. Don't make a fool of yourself."

I was making too much of it. I was simply taking this kind stranger up on his invitation to show me the city he was raised in and knew so well. No harm in that.

I quickly changed clothes, patted my makeup, threw a jacket over my shoulders and went to join Steve in the lobby. He took my arm and maneuvered me to the TKTS place, where we surveyed the marquee and settled for a Neil Simon play. We had a drink at Sardi's, and I felt I was in a play myself. Surely this couldn't be me!

After the play, we had dinner at Mama Leone's. Over a huge crab salad I got acquainted with Steve. He was unlike any man I'd ever known. His dark brown eyes sparkled as he regaled me with one story after another. We laughed until we cried. On top of all that fun, I was mistaken for Jessica Lange three times. Each time it got to be funnier, and of course the whole thing was quite flattering.

As the evening wore on, my attraction to this exciting man grew. Awkward feelings and strange new emotions started to play games with my mind. I kept telling myself that this was "just fun," but something was stirring deep within me. What in the world was wrong with me? I thought I would explode. It was obvious that Steve was experiencing similar emotions to mine. Not acknowledging any of it, we kept it light.

Steve retrieved his car from the parking lot at midnight and, not unlike Cinderella, I got into my coach. When we pulled up under the brilliant lights of the hotel's marquee, we kissed goodnight. It was nice! For a split second I toyed with the idea of asking Steve to my room,

~ ~ ~ ~ ~ ~ ~ ~ ~ ~ ~ ~ ~ ~ ~ ~ ~ ~ ~ ~

but good sense prevailed. Hesitatingly, I opened the door and clumsily stumbled out of the car. I was so deep in thought and engrossed with sorting out my feelings that I didn't notice the doorman holding the door. He finally cleared his throat discreetly. I turned to wave at Steve and watched him drive off into the warm May night. The party was over.

During the week I attended to the business at hand and spoke to Steve a few times on the telephone. We met on my last day in the city. I changed my return flight to a later one, so that I could spend a little more time with this Pied Piper. I felt guilty and bewildered when Gary picked me up at the airport. What was I thinking?

The next day, I had lunch with my good friend, Annette. She looked me straight in the eye and without hesitation said, "You met someone in New York, didn't you?"

I nearly choked on my fish chowder, gulped and managed a horrified, "How do you know?"

She frowned slightly, shook her head and replied, "It's as plain as the nose on your face." Just like that. Before I could come up with an answer, Annette asked, "What did Gary say? What are you going to do about it?

I shook my head in despair, "Gary doesn't know, and he won't ever know. I don't intend to do anything about it. I'm going to forget it, and you should too. For God's sake, don't tell anybody."

I hadn't planned any of it, and I tried to rationalize my emotion-drenched romantic interlude — brief and innocent as it was, I tried to make sense of my feelings. My giddiness must have been a result of the glamor of New York. I was charmed by a stranger — it had just been an innocent flirtation — I had needed something to bolster my femininity. I had proved to myself that men did find me attractive. As I

~ ~ ~ ~ ~ ~ ~ ~ ~ ~ ~ ~ ~ ~ ~ ~ ~ ~ ~ ~

brought things into proportion — sanity and sensibility survived. I came back to my life at hand, my work and my family.

When Steve returned to Portland, my lecture to myself flew out the window. We talked on the phone and met a few times, but the temptation to get involved was too great. I seriously considered having an all-out fling with him, but I couldn't go through with it. He was making me crazy. I had to bring the whole thing to a halt before it got a hell of a lot more complicated.

I met him for lunch, and told him firmly that I was committed to my marriage. I explained there was room for only one relationship in my life, and that I would not see him again. Steve was crushed. We talked about our relationship for a while, but I held my ground. We barely finished our lunch and sadly left the restaurant. As we walked into the sunshine, Steve said to me in parting, "If you ever get single, call me." I didn't see him again for nearly two years.

Several months after Gary and I were divorced and I was somewhat settled into the single life, I was having a glass of wine with my good friend, Pamela. We talked about this, that and the other, when she casually slipped in the question if I were dating anyone.

I told her that I wasn't seeing anybody and didn't know any men who appealed to me.

"You work with men all day long," Pamela said, looking squarely at me. "There must be somebody you'd like to go out with."

My thoughts immediately turned to Steve. "Well, there was this man I met on a flight to New York a couple of years ago. I liked him a lot, in fact. But that seems like a lifetime ago, Pamela. I totally forgot about him. I was really

~ ~ ~ ~ ~ ~ ~ ~ ~ ~ ~ ~ ~ ~ ~ ~ ~ ~ ~ ~

attracted to him at the time," I confessed out loud, as my mind conjured up his handsome face behind my eyes.

"Oh well," I continued, "he's probably happily married by now."

"Call him," Pamela instructed in her practical way.

Well, that was food for thought, and the next day, telling myself, "What the heck, what have I got to lose?" — I picked up the phone and called Steve.

Well, as fate would have it, he was not married and thrilled to hear from me. We met the following week, and it seemed that we were meant for each other. He was fun, outgoing, adventurous, and energetic.

Steve was ten years younger than I, and the idea of marriage was definitely not on my agenda. But after all the difficult times, the drama and the pain, and the ending of my marriage to Gary, it felt so good to be around a person who was so much fun, so passionate about life and full of laughter. I was enthralled.

Just to keep my head on straight, I approached this new relationship with a measure of caution and sanity. I limited our dating. Mark was still living at home. At the same time I had changed jobs from Touche Ross to Capital Trust.

I told Steve that my plate was full, and I would spend time with him on weekends, but not during the week. When he called me on a Wednesday afternoon, I made no bones about my displeasure.

"This is Wednesday! I thought I had told you to call me on the weekend not during the week. If you want to go out Saturday night, call me Saturday morning," and concluded the phone call with a hasty goodbye. Little did I know my independent manner only set the hook deeper.

Life was rich again. My new job with Capital Trust

~ ~ ~ ~ ~ ~ ~ ~ ~ ~ ~ ~ ~ ~ ~ ~ ~ ~ ~ ~

was blossoming into everything I had hoped it would, and my relationship with Steve could only be called blissful. It was several months later when I received a phone call from the national marketing partner at Touche Ross, who informed that he wanted me to move to their international offices in New York. He asked if I would consider heading up marketing for national accounts.

Great! I jumped at the offer. New York City — *Breakfast at Tiffany's.* I saw that movie when I was in college and always pictured myself living in New York. Audrey Hepburn, move over. I could be a blonde Holly Golightly with a few extra pounds.

I couldn't have been more excited. The timing was perfect. Mark was off to college in the fall, which left me free to do what I pleased. Lisa was living with her father and managing. I didn't think my moving to New York City would have an impact on her.

I couldn't wait to tell Steve and called him immediately. He wasn't around to take my call, and I left a message for him to call me immediately. It was important! Seconds later my phone rang, and someone on the other end said, "It's me."

Fairly exploding with excitement, I screamed, "You'll never guess who called me — Harvey Goddamn Braun! They want me in New York!"

Dead silence was the response.

I waited. Still no answer. Then a small voice said, "Karen, you wouldn't leave us, would you?"

Who is it? My heart raced. Then my heart sank. It was my new boss at Capital Trust! I recovered, laughed a bit too loud and said, "No, of course not. I was just excited for a minute. I'm staying right here. I love it here."

After hanging up the phone, I sat behind my big desk

~ ~ ~ ~ ~ ~ ~ ~ ~ ~ ~ ~ ~ ~ ~ ~ ~ ~ ~ ~

and banged my head against its hard surface, trying to knock some sense into it. When Steve did call, I lit into him like wildfire. "Why didn't you call sooner? Do you know what I've just done?" He roared with laughter at my crazy antics.

My talks with Touche Ross progressed, until I was certain of what I was going to do. New York City was it. Mark was going to college and busy with his life. I wasted no time, and put my house on the market. I was off to the Big Apple: "If I could make it there, I'd make anywhere...New York, New York." I couldn't wait.

It was a drizzly, grey Sunday morning in July of 1985, when Steve and I came to grips with the fact that I was leaving Portland. Steve's eyebrows rose, his face lit up and he said, "I can get a job with my old company. I'll move too!" He sounded relieved.

He was in the cement business and had been working for a Danish outfit when the company sent him to Eastern Oregon to build a cement plant. Once the assignment was complete, he stayed on with the client to help run the plant. Steve was a genius when it came to mathematics and was recognized in the industry for developing an expert system for operating a cement kiln. He could essentially write his own ticket.

Everything immediately fell into place for Steve. His former employer and friend rehired him on the spot, and before much time went by he was off to New York.

Unfortunately, my prospects for being transferred to New York had not only slowed down, they had come to a screeching halt. Acting on the premise that my future with Touche Ross lay in the East, I had sold my house. It was hard to let go of the past, but I was ready for a new life.

During this time, my friends at the Portland Touche

~ ~ ~ ~ ~ ~ ~ ~ ~ ~ ~ ~ ~ ~ ~ ~ ~ ~ ~ ~

Ross offices tipped me off that the firm was experiencing a great deal of internal difficulties. They advised me to play my cards close to my vest and not quit my job at Capital Trust. I took their advice. Before long, the managing partner of the international firm was deposed. The entire company seemed to be in a tailspin, and my New York prospects looked dimmer and dimmer. This was getting to be a familiar story with me and Touche Ross. Just when things were going the way I wanted, the partner-in-charge got fired.

I finally faced Harvey, and told him, "I have to move in two weeks. But I don't know if I'm moving across town or across the country. I need to know now," I insisted.

"I can't give you a binary answer," he replied.

I didn't know the meaning of "binary," but I knew that it would be "No thanks" for me. I think he was relieved to get me off his back. I never spoke to him again, and eventually the firm merged with Deloitte, Haskins & Sells. The Touche Ross I knew disappeared.

I was somewhat disappointed and at loose ends. Relying on the validity of the company's offer to move me to New York, I had initiated some drastic changes in my life, and Steve had changed jobs. He was now in New Jersey and I was still in Portland with no prospects of a job in New York. It was quite amusing and somewhat problematic.

Steve would call and say, "Why am I living in New York when I wanted to be in Portland, and you are in Portland wanting to be in New York? This is a fine mess you've gotten us into." He never stopped repeating those words in the eight years we knew each other.

We talked to each other every day commiserating about our situation, and he flew to Portland every other weekend. It was quite a commute for him — coast to coast.

~ ~ ~ ~ ~ ~ ~ ~ ~ ~ ~ ~ ~ ~ ~ ~ ~ ~ ~ ~

Brief as his visits were, I loved our weekends together.

Even though I was crazy about Steve with all his fun, laughter and exuberance, I was aware of the dark side of him. I had noticed Steve had quite a temper. The most charming man I had ever met exhibited terrorizing flashes of anger at the drop of a hat — or anything else for that matter.

There was the time during our early dating days when we had what I thought to be a minor disagreement on the way to the theatre. He became angry. Fires of rage danced in his dark eyes. In a voice I didn't recognize, he rasped, "Don't say one word until I tell you to." I caught my breath, gulped down the tears and didn't utter a word until he spoke to me during intermission. I never forgot how all-encompassing his anger was. I had not experienced anything like it since I left home.

It happened again, of course. I observed how he would became enraged with a ticketing agent or a parking attendant for things that seemed insignificant to me — just some common, daily annoyances most of us just live with. God help anyone who crossed him. I remember thinking what an ominous adversary he would make.

I also caught him not telling the truth from time to time. It was never anything very important, and I wondered why he lied about such little things. There were times when he would leave out relevant parts of a story or a plan he discussed with me. It was as though he rationed information and refused to give me the whole story at once. Eventually, this drove me crazy, because I never felt I played with a whole deck. He always managed to throw in the trump card of the missing information in order to gain an advantage. When I did mention this annoying trait to him, he merely laughed it off and said he didn't mean anything by it.

~ ~ ~ ~ ~ ~ ~ ~ ~ ~ ~ ~ ~ ~ ~ ~ ~ ~ ~ ~

Even though my stomach would tighten a lot, I chose to ignore the red flags — the signs of "danger ahead" — that dark side of him, because I was enthralled with his passion for life and his passion for me. He loved me like I had never been loved before — and it was wonderful.

Time flew by and the holidays were just around the corner when I drove to the airport once again to pick Steve up for his Christmas visit. He was going to spend the holidays with me in the charming condominium I was renting, right across the street from my office — just a short walk to downtown.

Bright Christmas lights and decorations lent a festive air to the otherwise gloomy, rain-soaked day. I love the season and was looking forward to Christmas with a childlike anticipation in spite of the unsettled life I was leading at the time. All that dropped away when Steve bounced off the plane and back into my life.

He was behind the wheel of my car driving home with the windshield wipers trying valiantly to keep ahead of the pouring rain. I was fiddling with a contact lens when Steve announced quite unceremoniously, "I know how we can solve our problem."

Still twiddling the contact lens absent-mindedly between my fingers, I asked, "How?" not really expecting any earth-shaking solution.

"We can get married," he said casually, never taking his eyes off the road.

I dropped my contact lens and never found it again. I had worn that same lens for thirty years and hated losing it. I looked all over the car, focusing on that bit of clear plastic. Finally, I straightened myself up, looked at his profile, and said, "Let's talk about it."

We settled in at my place, fixed ourselves a martini

~ ~ ~ ~ ~ ~ ~ ~ ~ ~ ~ ~ ~ ~ ~ ~ ~ ~ ~ ~

and talked about our future together. Needless to say, I told him I would marry him. That holiday was perfect.

It was a grand Christmas; it was full of magical moments. We laughed, we visited friends, we made love, but told no one about our plans. Besides, we really hadn't set a date. We just knew we would get married. Steve reminded me of a conversation we had about three months after we started to date.

We had been sitting in front of a glowing fire in my living room, when Steve said, "If I didn't think this would lead to marriage, I wouldn't be here."

Without hesitation I replied, "If you think I'm going to marry you, you are very much mistaken. You are ten years younger than I am, and besides, I've been married most of my life, and I have no intention of ever getting married again." And then I threw him out!

Well, that was then. I had a change of heart.

Steve returned to New York on New Year's Day but came back to Portland three weeks later. I had two tickets for a Trail Blazers game for the following Saturday but wasn't interested in using them. Instead, I called a travel agent friend of mine. "How hard would it be to get two tickets to Lake Tahoe just on the off chance Steve and I decide to get married?" I asked her without any preliminaries.

Annette replied with a cool, "No problem. Just let me know in the morning."

When I came home from work, Steve was waiting for me, and I got right down to basics. I gave him two choices, "Do you want to go to the Blazer game tomorrow night, or do you want to get married?"

His reply was something he often used and sounded something like: "Uh-Hum-A-Hum-A-Hum-A."

~ ~ ~ ~ ~ ~ ~ ~ ~ ~ ~ ~ ~ ~ ~ ~ ~ ~ ~ ~

"What does it mean?" I asked.

We looked at each other, grinned, giggled, burst out laughing, and said in unison: "Guess we'll miss the Blazers!"

That night we had dinner with friends of his. We told them we were getting married the next day and invited them to attend the celebration. But our friends had other plans and wished us good luck, the best and so on and so on.

The next morning we woke up early, and Steve, bless his dear heart, reached into his briefcase and came up with a dark-blue velvet box in his hand. All proper and groom-like, he got down on his knees and said, "Karen Halliday, will you marry me?" and presented me with a beautiful diamond in a Tiffany setting. Just what I had always wanted.

It was official; we were getting married.

We decided to fly to Lake Tahoe that day for a Nevada-style wedding. I called family and friends with my news and invited them to join us for the ceremony, short notice as it may have been.

Everyone was surprised. When I told my darling mother I was getting married, she recovered quickly and asked, "To whom?" Everyone but my sister Anne turned down our invitation to join us at Lake Tahoe. She laughed and simply said, "Karen, I wouldn't miss one of your weddings for the world."

Lake Tahoe was a true winter wonderland: white snow, blue skies, bright sun — just like the song, and quite a change from a wet and grey Oregon day in January. Our wedding ceremony was held at a place called Zephyr Cove, presided over by a minister who barely came up to my armpits. We enjoyed none of the touches of a well-planned wedding. The decorations were plastic, the music recorded, and my bouquet was made from the few flowers that origi-

~ ~ ~ ~ ~ ~ ~ ~ ~ ~ ~ ~ ~ ~ ~ ~ ~ ~ ~ ~

nated from a room service cheese tray — paper doily and all. Luckily, Anne had training as a florist, so it was nice.

We pulled up in front of the small building where we would be married. Steve turned off the motor, and I took a deep breath and let it out with a huge sigh. "Is this it?"

Steve looked at me and said, "Don't you want to go through with it?" I meekly nodded my assent. He reached for my hand, held my eyes with his and replied with deep emotion in his voice, "Karen, I wouldn't hurt you for the world," and got out of the car.

The service was short and sweet. I looked up at my new husband and saw nothing beyond the warm smile, and the laughter and the fun of the months past. The future held jealously onto its secrets.

Back in Portland, my good friend, Karen held a wedding reception for us. Steve raised his glass to make the toast, which began: "Some people live together and don't get married. We decided to get married and not live together." Perhaps we should have kept that arrangement.

I didn't mention my marriage at work. I needed time to figure out what I was going to do. It was obvious I was going to move to New York; I just didn't know when and under what circumstances. Steve and I saw each other as often as possible. I was busy at work. Steve was busy flying all over the country in his new sales job.

The old saying that "man plans and God laughs" once again proved its worth. What may have seemed a coincidence to some I believe was a sign of what I call grace. Spring arrived. Capital Trust sent me to New York to an investment conference. That trip couldn't have come at a more opportune time. During the conference, I ran into a recruiter, gave him my résumé, and told him I wanted to move to New York. He was a pleasant fellow and excited

~ ~ ~ ~ ~ ~ ~ ~ ~ ~ ~ ~ ~ ~ ~ ~ ~ ~ ~ ~

about the prospect of placing me. The bull market was raging, and I discovered that a good marketing person could get a job anywhere. Now it was my turn to be excited.

There was more of that magic in my corner. Within two weeks, the recruiter called me back to New York for several interviews he had arranged. What a lineup, indeed! I met with several top money management firms and banks, as well as Price Waterhouse. It seemed I could almost write my own ticket. I was shocked. Could it be that easy? I even had recruiters calling me after I returned to Portland. This was going to be a piece of cake. The future was mine. I was delighted.

By the time June rolled around, I had been interviewing all over New York, from Wall Street to Broadway. Of all the companies with which I met across the bargaining table, one stood out significantly. It was one of the leading money management firms in the world, and they wanted me! They made me an offer I couldn't resist. I accepted a job as vice president of marketing. The title was right, and the pay was good. My new job was to do what I had always done: set up a new department. This one would be dedicated to selling mutual funds in the institutional marketplace. I knew the 401(k) market, and mutual funds were the obvious investment choices.

Steve and I were thrilled that it had been so easy for me to find a position. He had purchased a small condo in Tenafly, New Jersey, near his office. I would move across country as soon as I could. It was not going to be easy to leave lifelong friends and family, but I felt this was what I was born to do. I never questioned it. It felt right.

Any doubts I had about my new job were overshadowed by my excitement. I couldn't wait to get started. I tearfully kissed Portland goodbye — I didn't know when I

~ ~ ~ ~ ~ ~ ~ ~ ~ ~ ~ ~ ~ ~ ~ ~ ~ ~ ~ ~

would be back. I missed Mark when he went away to school, but now I would be so far away from him. However, I was confident that I didn't have to worry about him; he would be just fine.

Leaving Lisa was another story. She was still fighting her battle with anorexia. The day I left for New York, she was once again in the hospital. I was scared — so scared. Yet I knew I couldn't help her any more in Portland than I could in New York City. But it seemed so far away. How could I leave her? I looked out of the window as the plane taxied for take-off from the Portland airport and prayed, "Dear God, please take care of Lisa and help her want to take of herself."

New York was buzzing with excitement and festivities when I arrived on the Fourth of July of 1986. Lee Iacocca and his committee had put on quite the show of shows in honor of the Bicentennial of the Statue of Liberty. Bunting and banners, flags and fireworks, parades and parties all contributed to the Independence Day celebration. I remember all the hoopla and flag-waving when I arrived, at which I bowed and said with mock humility, "All for me?"

I was in heaven. I had arrived in the center of the Universe and would be calling it home. Everything, just everything was happening in this city, this heartbeat of the nation. And I would be a part of it. I looked across at the CBS building where news was reported, where stars sang their songs, where famous actors said their lines and commentators brought the world to the front door of every hamlet and town in this country and the rest of the globe. Then there was Wall Street with all its power and money and greed and excitement — that place where fortunes were made and lost.

~ ~ ~ ~ ~ ~ ~ ~ ~ ~ ~ ~ ~ ~ ~ ~ ~ ~ ~ ~

I may have been far away from home, but in a sense I felt I had just come home.

July 1986

Dear Mother,

I'm having the time of my life. Everything available in the world can be bought here. People come in all different colors and speak all kinds of different languages. It's wonderful. Sensory overload prevails: the cacophony of sounds, the mingling of sights, smells; the people, the traffic, the construction — it's all amazing. I'm not a bit scared. I never know what I'm doing or where I'm going, but it's fun anyway.

People here are friendly, and I can't understand why they have such a bad reputation. I've not had one bad experience — except when someone asked me how I wanted my coffee, dark or light, and I replied "light" and was dismayed to find a cup full of milk and very little coffee. I'll learn!

The best thing is, I can always go home if I don't like it here — if anything goes wrong. I knew that when I moved to Portland twenty-four years ago. That takes the pressure off. I'm trying not to take myself too seriously and just have a good time.

The humidity is incredible. I feel like I'm going to fall flat on my face on the pavement the moment I step outside. Steve and I are having fun, but it is hard to have him gone Monday through Friday. It'll get better once I start to work and make some friends.

People are in a terrific hurry in the morning, so I try to go into town later in the day and avoid the rush. I like to fool around, get the lay of the land,

~ ~ ~ ~ ~ ~ ~ ~ ~ ~ ~ ~ ~ ~ ~ ~ ~ ~

and find out where everything is, before I start to
work. I don't want to be late my first day on the job!
Take care of yourself. Call me!
Love,
Karen
xoxoxo

LIFE LESSONS

ONE WOMAN

I was very much taken with Steve. After a twenty-year
marriage to Gary — steady as a rock — I was seduced by
Steve's passion for life. He was everything I wanted to be:
young, aggressive, exciting. I loved him dearly. He touched
my heart.

I felt a very strong connection to Steve from the very
beginning. It bothered me that he was ten years younger
than I am. But I decided it didn't really make any difference.
The biggest gap was in our taste in music. I had never heard
of Harry Chapin, and he could care less about Johnny
Mathis.

One thing did surprise me, though. I noticed the
minute we got married I turned into Betty Crocker. I bent
over backwards to take care of the house and my new
husband. He had been on his own for years, but all of a
sudden I felt the need to make sure he had a good meal on
the table and clean clothes in the bureau. The problem was
our jobs were equally demanding, but he would come home
from a hard day's work and catch a baseball game on TV
while I fixed dinner and cleaned the kitchen.

This lasted for a few months until I blew up at the

~ ~ ~ ~ ~ ~ ~ ~ ~ ~ ~ ~ ~ ~ ~ ~ ~ ~ ~ ~

injustice of it all. The funny thing was that he had no idea I was doing it for him. He said, "I didn't marry you because you are Betty Crocker."

It caught me off guard. I realized I equated being a wife with being a slave. It had nothing to do with him and everything to do with me and the old tapes that played around and around in my head. I realized my need to play the housewife role was self-imposed. I never really did get over it, but we worked together more from that time forward.

Steve was not exactly handy around the house, and that was all right. I wanted to experience New York, and I couldn't do that very well if I spent all my time doing chores around the house. I looked at everything I was doing to determine what was really important to me and what could go by the wayside. I hired a cleaning lady and called on Pedro, our maintenance man, to help me with other things. For the most part, it worked out pretty well. I also had to lower my standards a bit. That was the hardest part.

It might be good for you to take a look at how your time is spent.

- ☞ Are you spending too much time taking care of the people in your family? I had a sign on my refrigerator when the children were little that said, "What's best for the mother is best for the family in the long run." Think about it.
- ☞ How much time do you spend shopping, cleaning and cooking?
- ☞ Do you take time to nurture yourself?
- ☞ List ways you can take better care of yourself while caring for others.

~ ~ ~ ~ ~ ~ ~ ~ ~ ~ ~ ~ ~ ~ ~ ~ ~ ~ ~ ~

ONE LIFE

When I was interviewing for a job I visualized myself working for that person in that office, in that moment. I listened carefully to what my interviewer asked and responded with exactly what he had just told me he wanted me to say.

I also believed I would get a job offer. After all, that was the goal of my meeting, and I went to great lengths to help that person understand how much better things would be with me on his team.

The techniques listed below are to be applied once you are beyond the personnel officer and are interviewing with your potential boss.

- Sit down. Relax. Take a deep breath and smile.
- Appraise the situation before you speak.
- Get her to talk first.
- Ask questions and listen to the answers.
- Good questions to ask:
  - Who had this job before me?
  - What did you like about that person?
  - What did you dislike?
  - What are you trying to accomplish in your department?
  - What are the biggest roadblocks to your success?
  - Assume I am working for you in this position. How can I help?
  - How will you know if I'm successful?

Questions like these will help your interviewer make a human-to-human contact with you. Lean toward her. Help her understand her problem and how you can help. Try it the

~ ~ ~ ~ ~ ~ ~ ~ ~ ~ ~ ~ ~ ~ ~ ~ ~ ~ ~

next time you interview. What have you got to lose? And, as you leave, don't forget to "ask for the job." And keep in mind you are working for money. This is not a hobby. Ask to be paid what you are worth.

THE MONEY MYSTIQUE

From the very first year I started working, I invested the maximum into my Individual Retirement Account. Even though I thought I had a long-term, happy marriage, it was exciting to put away my own money.

I made a few ill-fated investments in "hot stocks" that brokers eagerly sold me. It took me six years to learn enough about the stock market to make informed investment choices that paid off. I lost every cent I put into stocks in my first years of investing. It's obvious I didn't know what I was doing. In fact, my inept investment method caused a knock-down, drag-out fight with Gary. It contributed to his despair. He couldn't believe I would buy stocks without asking him. I knew if I asked him, he would say no.

Of course, in retrospect, he would have saved me a considerable amount of money. I have learned that investing is a rational process, not an emotional one. Many women believe investing is like gambling. This is certainly true for people who invest without a plan. They might be better off to go to Las Vegas! There is no sense of urgency about getting into the market or getting out.

A few tips for the savvy investor:

The reason you invest is so your money can make money. Nobody gets rich by earning a wage. You need to have your money making money as well as yourself. Wealth is created through ownership. If you don't own investment

~ ~ ~ ~ ~ ~ ~ ~ ~ ~ ~ ~ ~ ~ ~ ~ ~ ~ ~ ~

real estate or a profitable company, you can benefit from ownership by buying stock in publicly held companies. Plan on having your money at work in the stock market for at least five years. For shorter time periods, save it; don't invest it.

The difference between saving and investing is simple. If you are sure you want your money back, then you save it. You save for things like a house, a car, a vacation, or to have a cushion in case of emergency. You put your money in a money market account or some short-term, safe place. And, if history repeats itself, you will indeed get your money back, after taxes and inflation. For example, assume you saved $100 in a money market account that earned you 5 percent for the year. At the end of the year you have $105. If you are in a 28 percent tax bracket. Your tax is $1.40. Inflation has been close to 3 percent for the past few years, so deduct another $3 for inflation. Your $100 is worth $100.60.

You can see you got your money back — just what you wanted. Just like Will Rogers said, "I don't want a

Initial deposit	$100.00
+ Annual interest earned @ 5%	5.00
Gross amount	$105.00
- Taxes on $5 @ 28%	1.40
- Inflation @ 3%	3.00
Net	$100.60

return *on* my money; I'd just like the return *of* my money."

On the other hand, if you want your money to make money and you have the time, don't save it; invest it. Historically, stocks have outperformed all other investments

~ ~ ~ ~ ~ ~ ~ ~ ~ ~ ~ ~ ~ ~ ~ ~ ~ ~ ~ ~

in any time period you measure. Read Jeremy Siegel's book, *Stocks for the Long Run,* if you don't believe me.

The problem is that people get scared when the market starts to go down, so they pull out…precisely at the wrong time. The idea is to buy low and sell high. What a concept! Studies show most people who invest on their own, without an investment advisor, invest emotionally. They buy in after the market goes up and sell out when it goes down. They don't have fun and they lose money. Then they have a bad attitude about the market.

- Decide what you want to accomplish with your investment dollars. Do you want your money to grow for use later, or do you need it to generate income right now? And remember, time is your best friend when you are investing. The longer the time frame, the more money your money can make.
- Draft an investment policy. This includes the time frame, the amount of investment dollars, the timing of the investments, and your anticipated return.
- Determine how you want your portfolio to look. Look at the various asset classes; cash, fixed income and stock, and decide what percentage of your portfolio you want in each.
- Narrow down each asset class until you decide what kind of bonds you want to own, or what types of companies. Do you want
  - government bonds,
  - municipal bonds,
  - corporate bonds
  - big companies

~ ~ ~ ~ ~ ~ ~ ~ ~ ~ ~ ~ ~ ~ ~ ~ ~ ~ ~ ~

- small companies,
- utility companies
- international companies

- Diversify, diversify, diversify. Don't put all your eggs in one basket. There are many types of companies to own, so you might want to invest in several types. Mutual funds offer wonderful diversification as well as professional money management.

- Once you have your portfolio in place, monitor it from month to month, quarter to quarter, or year to year. I prefer year to year because I know I am invested for the long term, and short-term ups and downs in my own portfolio don't interest me.

    I love the stock market almost as much as I love gardening, so I keep informed daily about the economy, interest rates, companies, and what is going on. I do, however, spend one day a year, when I do my taxes, re-evaluating my portfolio to make sure I am on track. I decide on any adjustments and make them throughout the year.

- Take your investments as seriously as you do your job. Look at them rationally, methodically and creatively. Investing is an art, not a science. And it's fun, once you get the hang of it.

- Taxes take a big bite out of investment returns. Your long-term investments should be tax-deferred, if possible. If you can invest for the future through an Individual Retirement Account or a qualified retirement plan through your work, so much the better. I've put money

~ ~ ~ ~ ~ ~ ~ ~ ~ ~ ~ ~ ~ ~ ~ ~ ~ ~ ~

away in an IRA every year since I started my first job. I've always invested in stocks through mutual funds. I've built quite a nice nest egg for myself over the years.

☞ Educate yourself about how the capital markets work. We fear what we don't know. You can create wealth for yourself by learning about yourself, your money, and the markets.

☞ Once you are educated, find yourself an investment advisor you trust. Don't expect her to be responsible for your investments; partner with her. Let her help you build for your future, but don't abdicate your personal responsibility.

Three cautions:
1. Don't ever invest in anything you don't fully understand.
2. Don't invest in anything because somebody else tells you to. Do your own research. Buying stocks, insurance, mutual funds or anything because your friend or brother-in-law is selling them is not a good reason!
3. Don't be impulsive; do your research first.

My salary increased considerably each time I moved to a new company, until my annual earnings approached six-figure status when I moved to New York. The more I made, the more I put away. It was thrilling to watch my investment portfolio grow. I could have bought more "stuff," but I was satisfied with what I had. It was a joy for me to put money away for my future.

~ ~ ~ ~ ~ ~ ~ ~ ~ ~ ~ ~ ~ ~ ~ ~ ~ ~ ~ ~

Learn to honor yourself by taking care of your money.

- Figure out what you own.
- Figure out how much you owe.
- Pay off all your consumer debt.
- Set specific financial goals.
- Keep track of how much you spend for three months.
- Make more money or spend less.
- Pay your bills on time.
- Plan ahead for purchases.
- Pay yourself out of each paycheck first.
- Invest for the long term.
- Invest in ownership by buying stocks.
- Educate yourself about money and the markets.
- Stay focused — no fear!
- Believe that no matter how limited your income and assets, you can provide a secure financial future for yourself.
- Take responsibility for your financial well-being.

CHAPTER
EIGHT

~ ~ ~ ~ ~ ~ ~ ~ ~ ~ ~ ~ ~ ~ ~ ~ ~ ~ ~

"Do not fear mistakes; there are none."
– Miles Davis

The first day at a new job can be nerve-wracking for anyone. I was excited, but I also felt apprehensive. I wondered if I could do what I was supposed to do. I wondered what kind of people I would be working with — they would know so much more than I did about everything: the company, the stock market, mutual funds. I wasn't familiar with New York City and would have to learn to find my way around. There were so many things I didn't know.

Even though I had met several times with my new boss, I wasn't sure exactly what my job was going to be. I had been handed a few mutual fund prospectuses, which I read again and again without real understanding. In spite of it all, it never occurred to me that I wouldn't know how to

~ ~ ~ ~ ~ ~ ~ ~ ~ ~ ~ ~ ~ ~ ~ ~ ~ ~ ~ ~

handle my new job. My friend Gloria told me once, "You're always chasing cars — now and then you catch one." I knew I had caught a big one!

The alarm went off at six o'clock that muggy August morning in New York, and I jumped out of bed. I chose a wonderful blue silk suit to wear with a pink long-sleeved blouse. One quick look in the mirror confirmed the wisdom of buying the best and taking care of it — I looked well-dressed for my new job with this international money management firm. Not only that, I would wear the suit for years. As always, I added some good jewelry and had a quick cup of coffee. In spite of being nervous, I felt good, and I was ready for my adventure. I think Steve was proud of me, and a bit of my excitement had rubbed off on him.

Steve left for work in New Jersey, while I headed in the opposite direction. The early morning was already hot and humid — so unlike Oregon — and the sticky, moist air clung to me like the ever-present fog in a steam bath. By the time I reached the bus stop, I was wondering how on earth I was going to survive summers in New York.

The bus ride to the Port Authority took an hour and a half, which gave me time to think and check out the other passengers. This was all new to me. I had seen scenes like this in movies, and all of a sudden, I was part of it — I was playing my role.

People buried their faces behind the pages of the *Wall Street Journal* or *The New York Times,* absorbed in the news, and paid little attention to their fellow passengers. I had brought a copy of the *Times* along, but between glances I peeked around to people-watch. I had never "commuted" to a job before and was quite curious — after all, I was going to spend a lot of time going from home to job and back again.

~ ~ ~ ~ ~ ~ ~ ~ ~ ~ ~ ~ ~ ~ ~ ~ ~ ~ ~

Pulling into the Port Authority was quite a sight. Buses and people were everywhere. Large crowds were surging, weaving and moving in every direction, hurrying to get ahead. Because of the problem with my knee, I held on tightly to the railing when I went down the steps that led to a lower platform. The high heels of my fashionable shoes slowed me down considerably. Impatient and rushing, eager to "get there faster," the jostling crowds passed me. I wasn't walking fast enough, and everybody was in such a damned hurry. (As long as I lived in New York, I never walked fast enough to keep up with the speed of the pedestrians.)

I glanced at the mile-a-minute-hurry-scurry throng of people as they zoomed and flew by me in a seemingly mindless pattern. However, I was certain they knew where they were going. I did not! I had not prepared well for finding my way to a new place. Several months had gone by since my initial interview with Alliance, and during that time the company had moved from Wall Street to midtown Manhattan. I had only been at their new offices once, and Steve had dropped me off at the front door. I had the address, but I had no idea where it was. I was truly a stranger in a strange city. I stopped several people and asked for directions to the subway. "Which way are you going, uptown or downtown?" they inquired.

I didn't have a clue where the Port Authority was located in relation to uptown or downtown. Was it uptown to downtown or was it downtown to uptown? It was all so confusing. I did learn a basic fact about New York: You've got to know whether you're headed uptown or downtown before you get on the subway. Among all these people, I just knew I was the only person who had no idea where she was or where she was going. Fortunately, my life experiences told me that I would get there — maybe not on time, but I

~ ~ ~ ~ ~ ~ ~ ~ ~ ~ ~ ~ ~ ~ ~ ~ ~ ~ ~

would get there eventually.

Tunnels like honeycombs loomed ahead. I started to walk down the tunnels on uneven concrete peppered with holes and unforgiving to the slim heels of my shoes. I was perspiring like a bricklayer. I could feel sweat running down my back. The silk of my blouse and suit were sticking to my skin like a warm, wet web. There was not a dry spot on me. My mind was numb with disbelief. How could I have made such a mistake? Why hadn't I done a dry run to my new job? What an idiot I was.

I had been rushing around the city for more than forty-five minutes, and I was late. I had walked and walked. Sometimes I went against the crowds, sometimes I moved with this river of people — so many people. Finally I was pointed in the right direction, when I told a passerby that I wanted to go to the Hilton Hotel, which was located directly across the street from the skyscraper that housed my new company

I had fiddled with my clothes so much, I knocked the button off my skirt. I was wearing a belt, but I knew the skirt would hang below it. Very attractive for my first day on the job! Trying to find a safety pin from street vendors in New York is a lot worse than looking for a needle in a haystack. They sell everything on the streets of Manhattan, except safety pins. Finally, I managed to get a safety pin at the Hilton Hotel lobby shop. Of course I had to buy a box of them which cost five dollars. (To this day I carry a safety pin in my wallet!)

That was the least of my worries. I was a total mess. I looked like hell! I had left home with my hair in place and looking good. Two hours later, the humidity had curled my hair into a big, bushy, unmanageable mess. My head and I couldn't fit in the same elevator. Perspiration had washed

~ ~ ~ ~ ~ ~ ~ ~ ~ ~ ~ ~ ~ ~ ~ ~ ~ ~ ~ ~

off my makeup. On the mezzanine of the Hilton, I located a small ladies' room. I wanted to see just what kind of damage control would restore the well-groomed look I had started out with in the early morning. It was hopeless.

I was drenched from head to toe with perspiration. I took off all my clothes. I stood in that tiny room in my bra and panties trying to dry myself off with paper towels while fresh perspiration continued to pour from my skin, making a joke of my efforts. I could not cool down. A few women dropped by to use the restroom. I just acted nonchalant, as if I did this every day — what's the big deal?

I held my sweat-soaked blouse under the hand dryer, but it was impossible to revive any part of my outfit to a semblance of well-groomed elegance. To make matters worse, the moist parts of my blouse were a different color than the dry ones.

In the end, I reluctantly put my wilted suit back on. One look in the mirror confirmed the fact that I was one big wrinkle. For someone who takes great pride in presenting herself well, for someone who thoroughly understands the importance of *presentation,* it was a nightmare come true. I never felt worse or looked worse in my whole life.

By the time I reached my new boss' office it was after ten o'clock. Not bad, just a little over an hour late! In the elevator, I pulled my shoulders back, patted my hair, plastered a smile on my face and told myself, "This is the worst commute you'll ever have. All the days to come will be a breeze compared to this day. Nice to get it over with." When the elevator doors opened and I stepped out on the fifty-seventh floor, I walked in as if I enjoyed arriving late, sopping wet, and wearing the biggest hair-do in town.

An older woman by the name of Miriam, who turned out to be my secretary, greeted me and gave me a curious

~ ~ ~ ~ ~ ~ ~ ~ ~ ~ ~ ~ ~ ~ ~ ~ ~ ~ ~ ~

look as she directed me to my boss' imposing corner office. I was mortified. Even though I was now navigating in air-conditioned comfort, I was still perspiring heavily. I just couldn't turn it off.

Our initial meeting, was quite brief. In order to lighten the situation, I tried to be funny and said, "I am sorry I'm late, but I had a little trouble getting here this morning. I guess I'm done now. I think it's time for me to go home. I feel that by just getting here I've done my job."

He did not crack a smile. He didn't think it was funny. A top executive hiring someone for a high-level position clearly expects that person to be on time and well groomed. Well, I was neither. Had I looked that way at my first interview, he would never have hired me. At that moment I was certain he didn't even recognize me.

I made as dignified a retreat from my boss' office as I could muster and went looking for Edna, who showed me around, pointing out the things I needed to know. The offices were imposing, almost intimidating, in their all-grey-and-black scheme. The furniture was made up of gorgeous custom-made pieces and covered in leather. Original black-and-white prints graced the walls, blending in with the decor, and an overall hush of "quiet, elegant affluence" prevailed in foyer, offices and hallways. It was quite a different atmosphere from the company's former Wall Street headquarters, which were less sterile, much more relaxed, a bit cluttered and a lot friendlier. The old offices felt more like me.

Then there was Miriam. My new secretary was a short, sturdy, dark-haired Jewish mother who turned out to be a whiz at her job. I don't know what I would have done without her; she would be my strongest source of support. She had been with the firm for years and knew the ropes.

~ ~ ~ ~ ~ ~ ~ ~ ~ ~ ~ ~ ~ ~ ~ ~ ~ ~ ~ ~

She helped me get along that first day. Tactfully, she never uttered a word about my disheveled state and, after a brief tour of the firm's two floors, took me to my fifty-seventh-floor office and left me on my own.

My quarters were furnished in the same posh style as the rest of the suites — grey and black with fine art gracing the walls. A big window offered a beautiful view of Central Park and the busy streets below, with their never-ending stream of people rushing to their destinations. An army of taxis formed a wide yellow ribbon that crept ever so slowly down Park Avenue — not getting anywhere fast.

When the door had fallen shut behind Edna, I felt isolated from the rest of my new world — the people at Alliance closed their doors. I gazed at the files and prospectuses on my desk, but I couldn't concentrate. I twirled my chair around, picked up the phone, and dialed Gloria's number in Washington.

"Gloria! Here I am sitting on top of the world looking down on Central Park. I've made it. Now what am I going to do?" I implored my old friend. "Remember," I went on, "when Sylvia with her MBA asked me how I thought I could move to New York because I didn't know anything? We laughed at the time, but I think she was right. How can I do this job?

Gloria, dear Gloria, just laughed. "Come on, Karen," she chided, "you've had bigger challenges. Get a grip."

We talked and laughed about my morning adventure — my commute from hell — and when I hung up, I thought, "She's right. I've had bigger challenges. So what if my clothes were destroyed, my hair looked like a fright wig, my makeup was shot, I didn't know anybody nor remotely how to do my job. On the other hand, here I am, forty-five years old, vice president of an international money management

~ ~ ~ ~ ~ ~ ~ ~ ~ ~ ~ ~ ~ ~ ~ ~ ~ ~ ~ ~

firm, with a good-sized salary and bonus. Not bad for a Raleigh Hills housewife."

My mind flashed back to the lunch I had with my boss and another senior vice president, shortly after I moved to New York, and a few weeks before I started my job. I had visited their elegant new offices that morning to complete my paperwork.

We went to lunch at the famous Jockey Club, which was another experience. Some of New York's "upper-crust" restaurants are really something. There are no loud neon signs or any other advertisements announcing their location. There is just a small, discreet brass plate buffed to a high polish gracing heavy wooden doors. The Jockey Club was a place to be seen — humming with lunch in progress when we arrived. It looked to me like everybody knew everybody.

We were seated in a big banquette, and my hosts recommended the lobster bisque. Go along, get along! Okay. I ordered the bisque. When my fancy soup arrived, I couldn't eat it. I was so nervous that my hand shook, and I couldn't get a spoonful of soup to my mouth. I have no idea why I was so nervous, but I learned a valuable lesson, always order an omelet when you're nervous. They're easy to eat — even a sandwich can be dangerous. I stick to omelets.

A few days after I reported to work, we went to lunch at another discreet restaurant. This time the fare was Italian. There were no omelettes on the menu, and I ordered angel hair pasta. I had never heard of angel hair pasta, but I liked the sound of it. My meal was great, and I ate it with relish. I was about halfway through with my lunch when I noticed that my companions were twirling their pasta expertly around their forks with the help of a spoon. I had been

~ ~ ~ ~ ~ ~ ~ ~ ~ ~ ~ ~ ~ ~ ~ ~ ~ ~ ~ ~

cutting mine with my knife and fork. Oh dear, another blunder! With my face a hot crimson, I picked up my big spoon and started twirling. It must take a lot of practice, because I twirled and twirled and couldn't get those slick little noodles to curl into a tight packet around my fork. I was chagrined, to say the least.

I went out that afternoon and bought a book on business etiquette. There was so much I didn't know. I read the book three times from cover to cover. It was the best investment I ever made. Thank you, Amy Vanderbilt!

As Gloria said, I had to "get a grip." Here I was in one of the most exciting cities in the world, had a job with one of the most prestigious money management firms — a job I really wanted — and I was fretting over something as silly as the decor of the office, worrying about eating soup and properly twirling a few strands of pasta around a fork. How utterly foolish. Why was I intimidated now? I never had been before. I knew I would do my job — I always had. However, this time I really didn't know how I would pull it off. Fretting wasn't going to get me anywhere; planning would, and I'd better get on with it.

Luck and timing were on my side. I knew my boss would be on vacation for the next month — starting on my second day. This was a gift from God which would give me time to get settled in and get down to business. Basically, my job was to sell the idea of mutual funds to the people who handled retirement plans for their organizations.

The first thing I had to do was to write my own business plan on how I would get the business — this I had done before. I had a whole month in which to do it. That wasn't scary to me. All I needed was a desk and a telephone and a little guidance from my boss to create whatever it was I was supposed to create. I had done that in my other jobs.

~ ~ ~ ~ ~ ~ ~ ~ ~ ~ ~ ~ ~ ~ ~ ~ ~ ~ ~ ~

The only difference was that this was all new to me, and the amount of learning I had to do was overwhelming, for the moment — not to mention the fact that my boss would be out of town. I was on my own.

I looked at my watch. It was almost five o'clock. My first day at the office had come to an end, and I would once again join the throng of people heading in the opposite direction — home.

Life Lessons

One Woman

I didn't plan ahead, which would have been the smart thing to do. I thought I could find my way easily. Neglecting to prepare set me off on the wrong foot, and it took me a while to recover.

- Always get the lay of the land. Pay attention to what goes on before you act.
- Take about six months to build personal alliances with people. You never know where the power really lies, and you will make mistakes if you move too quickly.
- When you are faced with a seemingly insurmountable challenge, take a deep breath, put your shoulders back, and smile. People do not know what you've been through, and they don't care. Your problems are your own. Don't burden co-workers with your tale of woe. Act as if you already have everything you want.

~ ~ ~ ~ ~ ~ ~ ~ ~ ~ ~ ~ ~ ~ ~ ~ ~ ~ ~ ~

ONE LIFE

The situation was scary to me. There I was with a great title, an excellent salary, and a beautiful office, and full of doubts about myself. Yet I have proven time and again that people believe you are who you say you are, and you can do what you say you can do. I still believed that it was a fluke I got to where I was. I still saw myself as that little girl from Bountiful, Utah, and was merely playing a role. It took me years to realize that the reason I did what I did was because I was willing to take the risk. I was willing to do whatever it took to learn a new business, and I never took no for answer.

Even now, I sometimes tell myself: "You don't deserve this, and when they really find out about you, they will know what a fraud you are." It's a daily struggle.

Make a list of your major accomplishments in life.
- What was your motivation?
- What made you feel successful?
- Do you feel you deserve your success? Why? Why not?
- How do you tell people who you are? By your appearance, your attitude, and by your willingness to learn new things and entertain new ideas?
- Do you speak up for yourself and hold your vision firmly in your mind? Or do you allow people to dictate who you are and what you can accomplish?
- Do you "show up" for yourself, or do you get scared and cancel?

~ ~ ~ ~ ~ ~ ~ ~ ~ ~ ~ ~ ~ ~ ~ ~ ~ ~ ~ ~

The Money Mystique

I made more money with every new job. I decided what I wanted to earn and asked for it. Negotiating for a good salary wasn't easy for me, because I was more inclined to say something like: "Oh, that's all right. I'll work like a dog, and you won't have to pay me very much."

It was a stroke of luck that I decided years earlier to start at a fairly high salary. It was also a good thing I asked to be a vice president. Once you have achieved a certain salary range and a prestigious title, it is much easier to continue up the ladder. I have not had a job where I didn't get more than my previous salary and an officer's title to match.

List your skills.

- Put a dollar value on what you know and what you can contribute to the bottom line of your company.
- If you are truly convinced of your value to your company, your bosses will believe you, but you have to show them by using your wits and your commitment.
- Find out what people in your position make at your company and at similar places.
- Map out a strategy for getting the salary you want and deserve.
- Every day on your way to work, tell yourself I deserve an income of $ _____.
- Create a collage of women who are successful and who are earning good money. Paste a picture of your face over that of one of the women. Look at the collage every day and thank God for your wonderful good fortune.

~ ~ ~ ~ ~ ~ ~ ~ ~ ~ ~ ~ ~ ~ ~ ~ ~ ~ ~ ~

- Read books on "negotiating" so you can negotiate the salary you want. You have nothing to lose and everything to gain. If you do not yet earn what you deserve, you will, if you persevere.
- Open your eyes to the opportunities around you. Don't get stuck in your little cubbyhole unless you are truly fulfilled and earn the money you deserve.

I have several women clients who come to me to help them cut their expenses, because they can't make ends meet. When we go over the figures, it becomes clear that these women are living on the edge of poverty. There's no place to cut. It often comes as a shock to them when I suggest they earn more money. We then look at their options and focus on ways to increase their income.

If you need to have more money coming in, get together with a few friends to discuss your goals and gather support. A Mastermind circle is perfect for this activity.

The first step is understanding how much money you want at a conscious level.

There is nothing wrong with wanting money. Money gives us options, choices, certain freedoms, and helps us enjoy life. We are meant to have abundance.

Go for it!

~ ~

CHAPTER
NINE

~ ~ ~ ~ ~ ~ ~ ~ ~ ~ ~ ~ ~ ~ ~ ~ ~ ~ ~

"Imagination is more important than knowledge."
  – Albert Einstein

Fall 1986

Dear Mother,

I've been here about three months now, and it's going pretty well. I'm not too thrilled about my job because my boss doesn't talk to me much. I still love the city and get such a charge out of it every single day. The biggest problem is Steve. He acted so weird when the kids came to visit last week. He actually got so angry while we were in the Village, he stomped across the street against the light, banging the hood of a car that honked at him to stop. I don't know what the deal is. It's almost like he's jealous of the kids or something. We haven't

~ ~ ~ ~ ~ ~ ~ ~ ~ ~ ~ ~ ~ ~ ~ ~ ~ ~ ~ ~

gotten off to the best start. I really don't know how to live with him He's wonderful one minute and screaming at me the next. I'm looking for things to get better. I hope things are looking up for you as well. I'll call you next week.

Love,
Karen
xoxoxo

Steve and I settled into a routine of sorts. Moving to New York was like moving to a foreign country. Everything was different — from pace to people. It proved to be quite an adjustment. The smallest project could become a major undertaking. We lived in Tenafly, New Jersey, for three months. Our home was a long way from Manhattan, and I was on the road at least three hours every day. I enjoyed being able to catch up on my reading during the long ride, and occasionally I'd strike up conversations with a fellow commuter. Our bus would chug through Bergen County, picking up professionals and working class alike. I never got over how hard people had to work and the long hours they had to put in just to make a living.

When Lisa and Mark came to visit, they accompanied me on my commute one morning just so I could introduce them to the madness called the Port Authority. It was quite an experience for them. All in all, we had a good time together, except for the fact that I was almost ashamed of some of our living conditions. We had cockroaches in our apartment. Horrors! I'd never seen a Roach Motel, but I was game — anything to get rid of those vile creatures. We didn't get much sunlight in our apartment, and there was no outside entrance or patio. I really understood how important

~ ~ ~ ~ ~ ~ ~ ~ ~ ~ ~ ~ ~ ~ ~ ~ ~ ~ ~ ~

having access to light and fresh air is to me. Matters of house and living, however, took a backseat to the happenings at my new job.

I was fascinated by the goings-on at Alliance. I couldn't believe I was a part of it all. It didn't take me long to figure out what I had to learn. For example, there was a meeting in the morning at nine o'clock Eastern Time. No matter where the portfolio managers or financial analysts were located, they were hooked up via telephone lines to the Sixth Avenue office. An operator would call roll: "London, Australia, Tokyo, San Francisco..." I was constantly struck by how many people had to be inconvenienced by the time differences. But there they were, all lined up like ducks in a shooting gallery.

In New York, the professionals were all seated around a huge conference table. The less-important people, like the marketing staff, were allowed to sit around the periphery of the big players on small gray leather banquettes. We didn't speak; we just listened. I never missed a meeting. This gave me a crash course in money management. I loved it.

The ritual began with the firm's economist giving his overview of what was happening in the economy. He discussed the "numbers," such as unemployment, retail sales, auto sales, inflation, consumer prices, and on and on. I was impressed with his knowledge. I understood very little of what was said at first, but I listened and took notes and asked questions later. My face still stings when I think of some of my dumb questions.

I clearly remember asking the manager of the bond department, "What does the PPI mean?" He looked down at me as if I had asked him to explain the Easter Bunny, and chillingly replied, "It's the inflation measure at the wholesale level." I guess he knew how much I didn't know.

~ ~ ~ ~ ~ ~ ~ ~ ~ ~ ~ ~ ~ ~ ~ ~ ~ ~ ~ ~

It took me years to understand what a basic question that was, but I'm still glad I asked. I stored away the answers. The more I asked, the more I learned; the more I learned, the better I could work. Fortunately, I was more concerned with learning than saving face.

On and on the meeting went. The financial analysts took their turns talking about specific industries, such as forest products, autos or retail. They would talk about businesses in general and then narrow it down to the goings-on at the specific companies they followed within a particular industry. The portfolio managers, who had to make the buy-and-sell decisions, asked questions. I was awestruck by how much they knew. After two weeks of this, I called Ralph at Capital Trust and breathlessly exclaimed, "Ralph, you've got to come here. You can't imagine how much information is available. It's in the air. All you have to do is breathe." I was ecstatic.

I also realized from that day forward I would never manage my own portfolio of individual stocks. No way could I compete with the big guys in choosing companies, knowing when to buy and, more importantly, when to sell. I've invested through mutual funds for the past ten years. Oh, I do believe you can make money by investing in individual stocks, but I believe you have to have the time, the interest and the skill. My friends who manage individual portfolios successfully spend as much as three or four hours a day at it. It's a job.

I drafted my marketing plan and started working my strategy. My boss rarely talked to me. He seemed preoccupied. He left a few months after I arrived for a position with another large firm in the industry. I was then reporting to another senior vice president, a dear man who had worked on Wall Street all his life. He was more interested in selling

~ ~ ~ ~ ~ ~ ~ ~ ~ ~ ~ ~ ~ ~ ~ ~ ~ ~ ~ ~

mutual funds through stockbrokers than to pension funds; consequently, he didn't pay much attention to me.

Meanwhile, the company hired several marketing people to work for the president, who had just returned from England to take over the firm's marketing function. He included me in his sales meetings, even though I was on the mutual fund side and the other marketers were on the bigger-plan side.

Easter 1987

Dear Mother,

Happy Easter! It's hard to be away during the holidays. I miss the kids and Anne and the family. Steve's huge family is wonderful and warm, but I still miss my own.

Steve and I still aren't getting along too well. He is so volatile, and I provoke him with the most minor infraction. I'm sort of getting used to the rhythm now, so I know when he is about to go into a rage. He'll get mad at somebody else, such as a ticket agent, his brother-in-law, or another driver. Then I know it's a matter of a few days or weeks before he is exploding at me. It's really hard. I don't know what to do because I love him, but it's pretty scary at times.

I'm sure I have a lot to do with it. I just wish I could figure out how to act so he doesn't get so mad. When I try to defend myself, he yells back, "If you don't like it, you should have stayed married to Gary. Get it through your head: I'm not Gary."

The kids are fine. As always, I'm worried about Lisa, but I have to trust she will manage on

~ ~ ~ ~ ~ ~ ~ ~ ~ ~ ~ ~ ~ ~ ~ ~ ~ ~ ~ ~

her own. I worry about you too. I'm sorry you are in so much pain. Wish I could help.

Love,

Karen

XOXOXO

Steve and I didn't know it, but our marriage was like one wild ride on a giant roller coaster. Each soaring high plummeted to frightening lows. I don't think either of us had any idea how to be married to each other. I expected him to be in some ways like Gary — easygoing, helpful and reliable. Steve in turn expected me to be a woman of the eighties — independent, sexy, and a money machine.

We had our first big battle as married folks over his leaving a suitcase full of clothes on the middle of the floor in the entry of our small apartment. I suggested that he put his clothes away before he left town again. To my shock and disbelief he raged at me endlessly. A string of words from "this is my house" to "get off my back" and other choice selections rained on me with the same force as blows to my body.

There were other things that kept us apart. Our values were not the same. Apparently, I was quite traditional. I valued a pretty home, nice meals, and lots of good conversation. Steve wanted to eat out, play tennis and watch the Yankees on television. Countless nights I wandered over to Tenafly — a cute little town full of unique stores — by myself, with tears streaming down my face, not knowing what to do. Everything seemed so difficult. My commute to the city was hellacious, my job was overwhelming, and my marriage was traumatic.

~ ~ ~ ~ ~ ~ ~ ~ ~ ~ ~ ~ ~ ~ ~ ~ ~ ~ ~

Yet there were the days when Steve would meet me at the bus all sunshine and laughter, and walk me home. On other nights he would have prepared a wonderful dinner accompanied by my favorite wine. There were mixed messages and conflicting signals — all of which confused me.

I still remember the moment the truth hit me. I can recall the very second I realized my situation with Steve was a duplication of my life at home. I had married my father.

Dad had been in town for an extended visit. A week after he left, I finally put two and two together. With great clarity I realized that in marrying Steve I had created the same situation in my marriage I had experienced in my parents' home. I saw how Gary was the antithesis of my father, while Steve was a replica of Dad. I somehow knew I would have to heal my past with Dad before I could have a fulfilling relationship with any man. I hoped I would make that peace while I was still with Steve. Until then, I had a disturbing feeling I would have hell to pay before I could sort it out.

Spring turned into a hot, humid summer, and people fled the city in droves. On weekends Steve and I would go for drives and explore the countryside. We visited his family and occasionally stopped by to see friends. Steve was clever, funny and entertaining. He had a good sense of humor, and we'd laugh our heads off.

We both enjoyed the theatre and rarely missed a Broadway play. New York was terrific. I always wondered just how long one had to live in the City to catch all it had to offer. From galleries to restaurants, museums, musical

~ ~ ~ ~ ~ ~ ~ ~ ~ ~ ~ ~ ~ ~ ~ ~ ~ ~ ~ ~

events, lectures, and more fine restaurants, I wanted to do it all. New vistas, different cultures, the old New York and the new Big Apple were an ever-changing kaleidoscope of sounds and tastes and smells. It was indescribable! That first year flew by.

The days got shorter, and finally the first week of fall 1987 brought a touch of crispness to the air and changed the colors of the landscape. Central Park turned gold and red and brown, and just like the song, "Autumn in New York"... it was lovely.

However, things at work were far from lovely, as they went from bad to worse. I couldn't figure out what was going on. Whether it's a big corporation, the friendly neighborhood bank or the White House, politics are practiced for personal glory regardless of far-reaching consequences for the rest of the players. Alliance was no different.

The senior officers seemed locked in a tug-of-war. It didn't have much to do with me, except I found it almost impossible to be successful because I didn't have support from any quarter. I felt like I was sitting on a powder keg on top of a volcano, and it was only a matter of time before it blew up. My instincts told me the marketing people were going to be seriously affected by the explosion and it wasn't going to be pretty. I was traveling for the company a lot by then and often missed the behind-the-scenes battles, but I was aware of their repercussions that lingered ghostlike in the fancy corporate halls.

In August, I had a busy weekend scheduled. I had to give a presentation in West Palm Beach early on Friday morning. Thursday afternoon, I grabbed my luggage, my briefcase, and my materials which were in a huge box, and hailed a taxi to race me to Newark airport for a five o'clock flight. The traffic through the Lincoln Tunnel was horren-

~ ~ ~ ~ ~ ~ ~ ~ ~ ~ ~ ~ ~ ~ ~ ~ ~ ~ ~

dous, and I didn't arrive at the gate until five minutes before my plane was to depart and learned, much to my dismay, I had been bumped.

I couldn't get another flight out that night unless I wanted to take a circuitous route through Atlanta. I spent all night getting to Fort Lauderdale. Once there, I had to drive to West Palm Beach, arriving at my luxury hotel about two o'clock in the morning. I checked in and let the bellboy take my luggage to my room.

The room was pleasant and the bed looked awfully inviting, but I still had work to do. I always practice before I give a presentation, no matter how little sleep I will get.

I unpacked my giant box of marketing materials and started going through the comb-bound books I intended to hand out to my audience in a few hours. Much to my dismay, my new secretary had screwed them all up. Some books didn't even have backs on them. I was furious. There was no way could I fix it. I practiced my presentation and fell into bed for a two-hour nap.

My early-morning audience chuckled knowingly as I regaled them with the events of the night before. They knew all about traffic holdups, missing a flight, and little sleep. They understood about the scrambled notebooks and graciously overlooked the mistakes. All in all, the meeting went well. Once my two-hour presentation was finished, I raced back to my room, changed my clothes into a pair of casual, stark white cotton pants, tee and jacket. I put on a pair of white espadrilles and tore out to the airport. I had promised Steve I would meet him in Portland at six o'clock that night for a special dinner he wanted me to attend. Luckily, I could make it because of the three-hour time difference.

Steve and I really did live in the fast lane. His territory

~ ~ ~ ~ ~ ~ ~ ~ ~ ~ ~ ~ ~ ~ ~ ~ ~ ~ ~ ~

was North America. Mine was the United States. We criss-crossed America like sunrise chasing sunset — sometimes meeting just for dinner and an evening together. I learned I could find anyplace I needed to find and go wherever I had to go. It was a great confidence builder for me. I always arrived where I needed to be and, with the exception of that first day I was always on time.

My luck didn't hold. I could see "delayed" notifica-tions on all the flights behind the airline counters. My internal radar was screaming, "This is not good." The attendant at the counter confirmed my suspicions. All flights were delayed due to weather conditions in the Midwest. My flight was bound for Chicago and then Portland. The new United Airlines terminal in Chicago was opening that very weekend, and I was anxious to see it. I asked if I could go through Dallas or something, whereupon the attendant said, "All flights are delayed in and out of Chicago. You won't miss your connection. Don't worry. You'll get to Portland on time."

I dutifully walked away, settled into a comfortable chair and read my book for a few hours until my flight was ready. The seat assigned to me in first class was right next to the door. A few hours into the flight, I noticed my shoe felt wet. To my surprise, the carpet all around me was soaked. The flight attendant explained with a false coloring of regret, "We ran into some weather on our layover in Chicago, and the rain came in while the plane was being serviced."

"Must have been quite a storm to soak the carpet," I shook my head in disbelief.

And with that I entered my own personal Twilight Zone. We approached Chicago in a battering rainstorm. In fact, the airport was so flooded it was an island unto itself,

~ ~ ~ ~ ~ ~ ~ ~ ~ ~ ~ ~ ~ ~ ~ ~ ~ ~ ~ ~

completely cut off from all traffic. If you were at the airport, you had to stay at the airport. As we got closer to the ground, I could see cars sitting in water up to their windows, and planes stranded all over the runways. My blood turned to ice as I realized it was going to be a long time before I got out of there. "Oh no," I thought, "What am I going to say to Steve?"

I was totally unprepared for the pandemonium inside the Chicago terminal. The new structure was still half-finished; the restaurants weren't open, the toilets weren't working, and the lines at the telephones were miles deep. People were rushing from hotel to hotel doubling and tripling up in rooms just to have a bed to sleep on. Children were screaming, parents cajoling, people were snoozing in awkward positions, while the airlines seemed paralyzed.

By now, the rubber soles on my espadrilles had come loose from sitting in water for hours and flipped and flopped annoyingly with every step I took. I was stumbling around like a waddling duck on a bed of rocks. I joined the flow of humanity looking for a hotel room, but there was no room in any inn. The phones were out of order, and I couldn't call Steve. I resigned myself to the inevitable and staked out a claim on a piece of the brand-new carpet in a boarding area.

I was a seasoned traveler and knew better than to check through my carry-on luggage with my makeup, my glasses and a change of underwear. Yet, I had been so tired from getting so little sleep, I had thrown caution to the wind and checked all my luggage through to Portland. All I had in my possession was my purse and my book, *Les Miserables* — how appropriate!

Sleep eluded me for the second night in a row. My contacts were scratching my eyes raw, but I couldn't remove them because I couldn't see without them, and I was

~ ~ ~ ~ ~ ~ ~ ~ ~ ~ ~ ~ ~ ~ ~ ~ ~ ~ ~ ~

afraid of losing them. The floor was hard and, much to my disgust, I realized the bar was open and people were medicating themselves with generous servings of cocktails. The night wasn't half over before roving bands of drunk people were screaming and laughing throughout the terminal. It was like Mardi Gras without the blues.

By morning, the airport had become approachable from the city, and the millions of us who spent the night in the terminal were joined by the millions who had flights out that Saturday morning. The scene resembled an invasion by the locusts. The terminal was about to burst at the seams from the overload of passengers hoping to leave Chicago. As it turned out, Friday night had been a non-event compared to Saturday morning.

I tried to spruce up as best I could. Wearing all white for traveling hadn't been the brightest idea. To say I looked wrinkled, wilted and worn out was an understatement. My shoes were a lost cause — walking in my bare feet was easier. I threw my dead shoes into my handbag and joined the throngs to get the hell out of Dodge.

But it was to no avail. I went from airline to airline and gate to gate trying to get on a flight. Three times, a ticket agent offered me a flight, I accepted, and when she punched in to confirm, the flight was gone. Finally, about noon, I joined the Red Carpet Club just to get away from the crowds. The telephones worked and I was able to get through to Steve. As soon as he came on the line, I was hysterical...sorry I missed the dinner, dead on my bare feet and in dire need of sleep. I just couldn't keep going. He laughed and said it was too late to cancel our weekend at the Oregon Coast and to let him know when I would arrive.

I approached the airline ticketing agent and asked her to get me a room at the Holiday Inn. To my delight, a room

~ ~ ~ ~ ~ ~ ~ ~ ~ ~ ~ ~ ~ ~ ~ ~ ~ ~ ~ ~

was available. I gratefully took the next bus bound for an overdue rest and a good meal.

I grabbed a packet of little fish crackers, a diet Coke, a toothbrush, and a small bottle of laundry detergent as I wound my way through the hotel lobby. Once inside my room, I breathed a sigh of relief, took off my clothes from the skin out and washed everything — my pants, top, jacket, my underwear, my hair, my teeth and my body. That shower was the highlight of my weekend. I set my clothes out to dry, wrapped myself in a bedsheet, and promptly fell asleep.

When I awoke late in the day, the sky was dark and I sat pondering my fate. "Here I am, a reasonably intelligent woman. So, why am I lying here stark naked in bed with only a sheet for cover? I'm starving, and I can't even call for room service because I have no clothes on. I've not only put myself out, but I've disappointed my husband. What the hell am I doing this for? Life's too short. I don't want to live like this anymore."

At that moment, I decided to return to New York and find another job.

It was not until Sunday that Steve met me at the United gate at the Portland airport just in time for me to walk him to American Airlines for his flight out. Fortunately, we could both laugh about our lost weekend — but it wasn't a real belly laugh. I was done.

I returned to New York and made plans to find a job with a firm where I would get support from its officers and which offered the kind of environment conducive to a saner lifestyle. The senior officers had not supported my efforts, rarely bothered to give pertinent information to successfully sell the company's services, nor did they consider marketing a valuable department.

I happily left my job at the end of September 1987.

~ ~ ~ ~ ~ ~ ~ ~ ~ ~ ~ ~ ~ ~ ~ ~ ~ ~ ~ ~

The bull market was in full swing, and jobs in the industry were a dime a dozen.

Christmas 1987

Dear Mother,

Found another job without too much trouble. I thought I might never find one after the market crash last October 19. I'm really excited about working for The Bank of New York. I have a good feeling about it. I can't start until I've taken a drug test and they've checked my references. The best part is they don't care that I don't have a degree.

Lisa is in the hospital this holiday. I used to freak out when she went to the hospital, but now I realize it is a sign of health. It is her way of taking care of herself. Good for her. I love her so much. Mark is coming for Christmas. Should be fun. Hope you all have a great time.

Love and hugs to everybody.

Love,

Karen

xoxoxo

Wall Street changed forever that October day. The market crash wasn't the only event. Michael Millkin, the junk bond king, was under suspicion, as was Ivan Boesky. Insider trading stories made daily banner headlines on the front page of *The New York Times* and the *New York Daily News*. Drexel, Burnham Lambert, the junk bond power-house, vanished overnight, and everybody was jittery. Those

~ ~ ~ ~ ~ ~ ~ ~ ~ ~ ~ ~ ~ ~ ~ ~ ~ ~ ~ ~

high-rolling Wall Street jobs just flew out the window. I met with several financial recruiters who were crying the blues. One prominent player leveled with me. "Listen, Karen, you're going to have a hell of a time finding a job." I shot back, "I only need one, and I'd like your help."

By now, I'd told Steve and everyone else I didn't have a college degree. For most of my life and career, I skirted the issue as much as possible. I had wanted to go back to school for years but couldn't because I would have had to admit I hadn't finished years ago. People just assumed I had — and I let them. It really limited me. Besides, I felt awful anytime the subject came up. I was ashamed for not graduating. Now I was free to go back to school. I attended Marymount Manhattan College and took night classes. It wasn't that easy. The nights I attended class I'd get home at midnight. It was almost like the old college days, where getting enough sleep was not an option.

Winter 1988

Dear Mother,

It's so much fun to be back in school. I'm taking all sorts of classes: economics, trust and estate law, philosophy, accounting. I love it all. Here I am working side by side with MBAs from the best schools, and I'm taking ninth-grade algebra. It's a struggle, but funny as it may seem, I can usually get the answers by intuition. Then it takes me forever to figure out the formula.

It is so hard. I study every weekend for hours and practically wind up in tears. If it weren't for Steve, I wouldn't be able to do it. He is a mathematical genius, thank God. He even went to an

~ ~ ~ ~ ~ ~ ~ ~ ~ ~ ~ ~ ~ ~ ~ ~ ~ ~ ~ ~

accounting class for me while I was out of town. He eats this stuff up. I do too. I want to know it, but it's such a stretch. Was I always terrible at math, or did I learn to be terrible because I'm a girl? Interesting question.

I get good grades because I study like crazy. I know I can do it. I just have to lay down tracks in my brain for this stuff to stick. It always goes in one ear and out the other. This time I'm going to make it stick. Wish me luck.

Love,
Karen
xoxoxo

Ah, The Bank of New York. What a wonderful transition. Nice people, easy to get to know. And they accepted me from the very first day. My job was a delight. I had to work with other bankers and their clients to provide them with money management services. I knew I could do it without question. At last I had enough experience to do a good job right from the start. Sure, I didn't know much about trusts and estates, and I didn't know anything about municipal bonds, but compared to where I'd been before, it was easy. What I loved the most was the feeling of being accepted by everyone around me.

Spring 1988

Dear Mother,

The bank has started a hostile takeover of Irving Bank & Trust. It's really interesting to see how they play hardball around here, in such a genteel

~ ~ ~ ~ ~ ~ ~ ~ ~ ~ ~ ~ ~ ~ ~ ~ ~ ~ ~ ~

fashion. People refer to me as Miss Halliday, not Karen. It's a different world. Carter Bacot, the firm's CEO, takes no prisoners. He's pretty impressive, and I would put my money on The Bank of New York.

I do love my job. People are very receptive and include me in client meetings. It couldn't be going better. It's so much fun to work with wealthy people. I mean *serious wealth.*

Yesterday, I called on a woman in her Park Avenue apartment. Her entire place was decorated with original masterpieces: Van Gogh, Matisse, and a haunting El Greco.

But there seems to be such fear among the women about what to do with their money. This same woman, worth millions of dollars, sent her maid out on an errand while I was there. When the maid returned, she made her go over the sales slip and count out the change from a ten-dollar bill. What madness. I see it every day — and not just with women.

A man with a net worth of more than seventy million dollars has a fit if he gets charged one dollar at the ATM. Give me a break. Wealthy people are just as whacked out about money as those without any money at all. I would like to find a way to help people feel more at ease with their money. Money should be enjoyed, but most people live in fear of it. As Auntie Mame said, "Life is a banquet, and most poor fools are starving to death." Hope you feel better. My love to Willard. Miss you.

Love,
Karen
xoxoxo

~ ~ ~ ~ ~ ~ ~ ~ ~ ~ ~ ~ ~ ~ ~ ~ ~ ~ ~ ~

Winter 1989

Dear Mother,

The unthinkable has happened. I fell down outside Grand Central Station last week and right on my poor knee. I was in terrible pain. Steve had to come get me.

I'm so scared. What if I have to quit my job? Everything is going so well after the merger. I'm moving to midtown offices, where I will have marketing responsibility for the bank branches in Manhattan and Long Island. I have several people reporting to me. I have a new boss who used to be with Irving Trust. The jury's still out on him, but I don't want to leave.

I'm going to stick it out as long as I can. It's just so hard to get around here. I fall down regularly now, particularly at the Port Authority. Really stops the rush-hour traffic. One day, my shoes actually flew off as I fell with a thud. I'll let you know what happens.

Take good care.

Love,
Karen
xoxoxo

Once again, my knee became my nemesis. I wanted to scream and run out of the room when the famous knee surgeon told me, "You can only have one artificial joint because there isn't enough bone left to attach more than

~ ~ ~ ~ ~ ~ ~ ~ ~ ~ ~ ~ ~ ~ ~ ~ ~ ~ ~ ~

one. New joints wear out in active people like you. So, don't even think about it for another twenty years." In shock, I meekly asked, "What should I do?" His answer, "You'll have to change your lifestyle so your knee will last as long as you do."

Stunned, I left the clinic. I tried to make do by wearing a huge leg brace; cobalt blue, cumbersome with lots of velcro, which ripped my pantyhose. What a nuisance it was to slap on the brace, haul myself over to the subway, grapple for a seat, hobble to a hotel restroom, remove the brace, throw it in a bag and arrive for my appointment smiling and ready to go.

After a few months, I started the wheels in motion to return to Portland. It broke my heart, but I felt I had no choice. I could stay there, destroy my knee and eventually leave New York, or I could leave New York with my knee still intact. I may never take no for an answer, but I am adept at cutting my losses.

July 1989

Dear Mother,

When Lisa paged me in the Red Carpet Room to tell me you didn't wake up last night, I couldn't believe it. The other passengers squirmed in their seats as I screamed into the phone, "What do you mean she died? What are you telling me?"

Here we were, on our way back home, and I was looking forward to spending more time with you. I can't believe you're never going to call me again – that I'm never going to talk with you. What an odd idea.

All these years you gave me so many gifts.

~ ~ ~ ~ ~ ~ ~ ~ ~ ~ ~ ~ ~ ~ ~ ~ ~ ~ ~

Now I feel alone, lost. I question life, death and what's it all about? I have no answers. I admire you so much. You had the courage to divorce my father — so many heartaches.

Anne, Patti, Diana and I had a good time dressing you for the last time and putting on your makeup. It brought the four of us very close, and it felt like a loving thing to do. You did look pretty funny lying stone-cold on the gurney with your hair up in rollers. We laughed until the tears streamed down our faces. I know you got a kick out of it too. I can just see you giggling now.

We sent you off with pretty soft brown eyeshadow, pink lips, and I painted every single eyelash individually with your own mascara. Your hair looked fabulous. We sprayed you with Chloe so you smelled like you, and put a pretty crocheted hankie in one hand, a rose in the other — to cover up your bruises.

You were beautiful. Covering your face for the last time seemed so final. I know you will always be with me in spirit, but I was devastated. Who is going to laugh at my stories? Who is going to tell me I am wonderful when I don't feel wonderful? Who is going to celebrate my successes and talk me out of my failures?

I'm so happy I flew to Sun City to see you on Mother's Day. I had a feeling you were going to be giving up your body soon, and I wanted to see your new place and visit with you one last time. It was the best Mother's Day ever.

Thank you for loving me and believing in me. I'll drop by the cemetery when I'm in Salt Lake. You've got a beautiful view of the Wasatch Mountains and plenty of sunshine and shade. And

~ ~ ~ ~ ~ ~ ~ ~ ~ ~ ~ ~ ~ ~ ~ ~ ~ ~ ~ ~

I'm sure your sisters and grandma and grandpa are happy to have you resting beside them.
Take good care,
I love you,
Karen
xoxoxo

Life with Steve still had its ups and downs; we went from bliss to battle. Moving day was unforgettable. By then Lisa was living with us, mother's funeral was a month past, Steve was leaving his job, and emotions ran high. We were exited and sad at the same time.

The day began with the movers arriving late. We had reserved the elevator in our apartment building for the morning, but by the time they arrived, we had lost the sole use of the elevator. To make matters worse, the movers were the most surly threesome I'd ever met, and working with them would prove to be as big a challenge as the whole move.

Next, the moving van turned out to be too small to hold our belongings. A hasty call to the moving company resulted in an auxiliary truck arriving three hours later to hold the overflow. However, all our stuff would end up eventually being transferred to another van destined to haul it all cross-country. If that wasn't bad enough, just when all our furniture was scattered over the loading dock, it started to rain.

I just about lost it. In fact, I wasn't in the best mood all day long. I don't know what it was all about. Was I sad to leave Lisa, who was just moving to New Jersey while we were heading West again? Was I still upset about Mother's

~ ~ ~ ~ ~ ~ ~ ~ ~ ~ ~ ~ ~ ~ ~ ~ ~ ~ ~

death? Did I feel badly about leaving my job at The Bank of New York? Or did I mourn giving up our beautiful apartment with its spectacular corner view of Manhattan and the glitter of New York? Whether it was one thing bothering me, or all of them crashing in on me at the same time, I was less than charming.

By nightfall Steve and I were barely speaking. He thought I behaved poorly all day. (I must say he was right.) I had been pretty emotional and close to tears all day. As far as I was concerned, no one was doing anything right. Steve had tried to cheer me up and make me happy, but when that didn't work, he was really angry.

When we closed the last suitcase, I asked him to carry something for me. He erupted like Mount Vesuvius on a bad day. "I'm sick and tired of taking care of you," he yelled. "Go to hell," he shouted as he jammed his suitcase shut, stormed down the hall, left the apartment and slammed the door behind him.

I stood in the middle of the bare rooms, feeling empty and bewildered. I tried to figure out what to do, fully believing that Steve would drive to the airport without me. I swallowed hard, fought back the tears and wandered slowly through the vacant rooms saying a lonely goodbye to the walls that had been home to me for a while, and to the city — that part of my "dream-come-true" fairytale.

The bright lights of the city winked at me and seemed to reflect my sadness and pain back to me. My life in the fast lane had come to an end, and maybe I would have to live the rest of it by myself. I grabbed my suitcases, squared my shoulders and closed the door gently behind me. No use to slam the door shut on the past — it could be opened with just the wink of a thought.

~ ~ ~ ~ ~ ~ ~ ~ ~ ~ ~ ~ ~ ~ ~ ~ ~ ~ ~ ~

When I stepped out onto the sidewalk, Steve was sitting behind the wheel of the car waiting for me. I didn't even glance at him as I settled into the passenger seat. We drove all the way to the Holiday Inn near the airport in a cold and stony silence. I was leaving for Salt Lake City, and he was traveling to Portland. We never said another word to each other — two people going in the same directions on different paths.

Two days later, Steve called me to apologize. I'm not sure who needed to apologize. My behavior that day had been less than gracious. I believe I saw myself clearly as I held up the mirror of honest self-appraisal that night.

Eventually, like all the hundreds of arguments Steve and I had before, we kissed and made up.

LIFE LESSONS

ONE WOMAN

In May of 1989, I was sitting at my desk at 48 Wall Street when I picked up the telephone and called my friend Elaine in San Diego. "Elaine," I said, "I have this terrible feeling Mother is going to die. I'm not going to come see you next week; I've got to got to Sun City and see mother for the last time."

I don't know how I knew. I just knew that my mother was going to leave us. She had been living in constant pain from various kinds of arthritis and was near the end. She bruised if she brushed by a doorknob; her bones were as brittle as matchsticks from years of taking prednisone, and her ribs were beginning to crack regularly. Every movement

~ ~ ~ ~ ~ ~ ~ ~ ~ ~ ~ ~ ~ ~ ~ ~ ~ ~ ~ ~

hurt; she couldn't smile without pain. Yet she always looked like a million bucks.

When I kissed her goodbye at the airport after five wonderful days, I knew I would never see her again. Tears streamed down my cheeks all the way back to New York. I kept telling myself, "You have to let her go." In spite of all my "knowing," her death shocked me for two reasons: One, she was really gone; and two, my premonition was right.

In retrospect, I wish I had talked with my mother more, asked more questions. As I grow older, I realize the tremendous courage she had to face her challenges head on. She was plagued with arthritis for twenty-five years, yet she took extraordinary care of herself. She didn't like the puffiness from the prednisone, but everyone she met commented on her remarkable beauty. It came from the inside out.

My mother had courage in spades. She divorced my dad after twenty-eight years of marriage. In 1963, that was a no-no, particularly in a small Mormon community. Many of her friends fell by the wayside. She received little or no support from her parents. Money was tight, to say the least. In spite of it all, she found herself a job she enjoyed. She made new friends. And eventually built a new life for herself with my stepfather, Willard. Her house was always immaculate and charming.

I think what carried her through was her ability to laugh at life and at herself. Maybe courage is about being able to laugh at yourself. I see many women who take themselves so seriously. They characterize mistakes as failures. They are afraid to step out into the light. They are afraid of themselves and their own power.

It takes courage to cut your losses. It takes courage to say to someone, "This isn't working very well for me." It

~ ~ ~ ~ ~ ~ ~ ~ ~ ~ ~ ~ ~ ~ ~ ~ ~ ~ ~

takes courage to stand firm in your convictions. And it takes courage to take responsibility for yourself.

- Think of a time when you found the courage to tell someone how you truly felt. What happened? How did you feel?
- Do you have the courage to do what you know is right, even if you are afraid? Ask yourself, "What is the worst that can happen?"
- Then tell yourself you can always change your mind. The only irrevocable decision I know about is the decision to have a child. Otherwise, you can always change your mind, pick up the pieces, and move on.
- And what about listening to your inner voice? We all have an inner voice that talks to us, but most of us choose not to listen.
- How many times has your inner voice told you to do something and it turned out to be right?
- Slow down and quiet your mind every day and go within to a place of silence. Listen to your inspired insights.
- Act upon them.
- Notice how much smoother your life goes when you live in accordance with your higher self (your inner voice).

ONE LIFE

Marriage to Steve was difficult. Our backgrounds, motivations and values were constantly at odds. I couldn't communicate my needs to him, and he couldn't communicate his needs to me. His verbal abuse made me feel less and

~ ~ ~ ~ ~ ~ ~ ~ ~ ~ ~ ~ ~ ~ ~ ~ ~ ~ ~

less capable. Several times during those first few years I wanted to leave him, but I didn't know how. Marriage is a commitment, and I loved him. I couldn't admit, even to myself, how unhappy I was much of the time. As the years passed, we spent less and less leisure time together. I wanted to go into the city on the weekends. He wanted to play tennis. I'd wander around Central Park by myself, looking longingly at the couples strolling hand in hand.

I saw a therapist, Mrs. Jackson — a darling little woman — every week in New York. She was in her late seventies, and just what I needed. She had to use a footstool because her legs were so short they didn't reach the floor. She would close her eyes, cross her arms over her stomach, sigh, and ask me, "What do you think you are proving by staying with Steve? Aren't you lonely?" I'd always nod in affirmation, but I felt powerless to help myself. I knew if I could change enough, I could make him stop getting angry with me.

If you're in a situation with a partner who is abusing you, do whatever you can to break the cycle of abuse. Verbal abuse is as damaging to the spirit as physical abuse is to the body.

If all else, fails, give no for an answer, cut your losses and get out.

THE MONEY MYSTIQUE

Working with wealthy people gave me a valuable lesson about money. I grew up with the impression that rich people were happy people. I found this wasn't necessarily true. So many of my clients were afraid of investing, afraid of spending, afraid of losing their money. I met very few people who were at ease with their wealth unless they were

~ ~ ~ ~ ~ ~ ~ ~ ~ ~ ~ ~ ~ ~ ~ ~ ~ ~ ~ ~

old money or, as they say in New York, "white-shoe money." But those people had a different problem. They had to preserve the family wealth, so they weren't free to express themselves in all their magnificence either.

My motto is Money — create it, spend it, invest it, enjoy it. Money is a form of energy that we exchange for goods and services. It flows in and out of our lives regularly. I believe the first step to feeling at ease with money is to recognize there is enough for everybody. Abundance is a natural law of the Universe, and if we are conscious about how we create our money, how we spend our money, and how we invest our money, we will enjoy our money and consequently our lives.

Money has no value as an object in itself. It is only valuable as a means of exchange. When we are in the money flow, we know it. There are wonderful books on the subject. Pick up a copy of *Creating Money* by Duane Packer and Sanaya Roman. There are as many books on the metaphysical aspect of money as there are on the physical aspect of money. The challenge is to bridge the gap from creating money by being with it in a healthy way and consciously investing money so it works for you.

Answer the following:
- What are your money secrets?
- What would people be surprised to know about you and your money?
- When the subject of money comes up, how do you feel?
- Describe what it's like for you to talk with your friends and family about money.
- Describe how you feel about buying things for yourself.

~ ~ ~ ~ ~ ~ ~ ~ ~ ~ ~ ~ ~ ~ ~ ~ ~ ~ ~ ~

- What brings you the most happiness? How often do you do it?
- What do you like best about the way you handle money?
- What do you like least about the way you handle money?
- Describe how you spend money. (Do you write down what you spend? Do you spend until it's gone? Do you keep track of it in your head?)
- What was your last major purchase?
- What need did it fill? How did you pay for it?
- What are you dreaming of buying now? How will you feel when you get it?

CHAPTER
TEN

~ ~ ~ ~ ~ ~ ~ ~ ~ ~ ~ ~ ~ ~ ~ ~ ~ ~ ~

*"Courage doesn't always roar. Sometimes
courage is the quiet voice at the end of the
day saying, 'I will try again tomorrow.'"*
– Mary Anne Radmacher Hershey

I settled back comfortably into the routine of Portland:
friends, family and Capital Trust. It was nice to be in
familiar surroundings again. We found our dream house and
furnished it together. We created a home we both loved.

I did miss the excitement of New York, the theater, my
new friends, and Wall Street. Mother's death hit me pretty
hard, and I spent a long time grieving over my loss. With the
realization of that loss, I experienced such an emptiness, a
feeling of a bottomless loneliness, and quite a drain on my
energy.

In the meantime, I started working on my issues with

~ ~ ~ ~ ~ ~ ~ ~ ~ ~ ~ ~ ~ ~ ~ ~ ~ ~ ~ ~

my dad. When I was still in New York and seeing Mrs. Jackson, she helped me understand that I had recreated my relationship with my father in my marriage to Steve. She also led me to believe the only way I could enjoy a healthy relationship with a man was by confronting my problems with my father.

My dad visited us in New York shortly before we returned to Portland. He said something that angered me, and I flew into a rage and blasted him for everything he had done to me. It wasn't a pretty moment. Steve walked in during my tirade, told me to quiet down — he had heard me screaming all the way down the hall. I stopped yelling but was still seething on the inside. Once I let the genie out of the bottle, I couldn't get it back in.

My father was furious with me and didn't speak to me for two years. About a year later, I tried to mend fences and wrote him a letter explaining my point of view. He replied with a scathing epistle, calling me names, referring to me as a "screaming harridan." He dressed me down for everything he considered an infraction of mine since I was born. In his eyes, I had done nothing right. Tit for tat. And, to further humiliate me, he sent copies of his letter to my brother, my two sisters, his sister and to Lisa. I don't know why he spared Mark, but I was grateful.

August 1990

Dear Mrs. Jackson,

You were right. I did need to work on my relationship with my dad. It's taken a terrible turn and I don't feel very hopeful. Steve is still his old irrational self; angry one minute and loving the next. I feel like I'm going crazy.

~ ~ ~ ~ ~ ~ ~ ~ ~ ~ ~ ~ ~ ~ ~ ~ ~ ~ ~ ~

My job at Capital Trust didn't work out very well, either. I left last June with nothing much planned. Mother's death and Dad's anger have really hit me hard. I need time to just be. I have been so busy "doing" for so many years, I'm going to do something about just "being" for a while.

Steve initially agreed to support me while I took classes to become a certified financial planner. That lasted for one month, and the situation became a problem for him. He resents my not making money. I wanted to start my own company teaching women about money, when he challenged my plan, and said, "How can you teach anybody about managing money? You're too dumb in math." I know he is right. I put that dream on hold or, as he says, "Send that play back to the bench." I'm feeling less and less happy in the marriage. The conflict gets to me.

I will get my degree this year. At least I'm not too dumb to go to school.

Thanks for your nice card. I appreciate your support. You've been a great friend.

Take care,
Karen

I spent the next year close to home. I went back to school at Marylhurst College and worked toward a degree in communication. It was easy because I had taken so many classes and had more than enough hours. I just needed to have forty-five hours at Marylhurst and I could finally, at long last, get my degree.

The communication classes were excellent. These studies gave me a chance to better understand personal

~ ~ ~ ~ ~ ~ ~ ~ ~ ~ ~ ~ ~ ~ ~ ~ ~ ~ ~

communication and conflict management, as well as male-female communication. I really applied myself in an attempt to better communicate with Steve.

I enjoyed being home more. We bought a beautiful house in a lovely old part of Portland. It was the kind of neighborhood where the oak trees reached out to the opposite side of the street and met in the middle. The flowers changed with the seasons, and the lawns were green all year long. This was truly my dream house — all one level so I could get around, beautiful brand-new raspberry carpet, and gleaming white appliances in the kitchen. I hadn't had a chance to nest for years and it felt so good to just be home.

I kept busy. In addition to school, I studied for and passed three of the six Certified Financial Planner exams. Life was good. Lisa was thriving in New York. She graduated summa cum laude from Fairleigh Dickinson University and was happy. Mark was busy in his first job with a public relations firm and buying and fixing up old houses to earn money on the side. I continued in therapy, trying to come to grips with my own anger, and more than that — how to live with Steve's.

Steve gave me a hard time about not working. He didn't understand I was going through a really deep grieving process. I was grieving for my mother, for my father, for Lisa, for Gary, and for my marriage. On numerous occasions he suggested that I go back to work since I was so unhappy at home. He couldn't understand that I needed to spend time in solitude. All he understood was the fact that, for once, I was not earning any money. He didn't like that.

On Mark's birthday in 1990, I happened to be wearing a pair of grubby jeans and a white sweatshirt — not exactly

~ ~ ~ ~ ~ ~ ~ ~ ~ ~ ~ ~ ~ ~ ~ ~ ~ ~ ~ ~

dressed for success — when Steve turned to me and said, "Just look at you. Look at what you have become. I can't believe you are the woman I married. How can you stand yourself? You're nothing but a big disappointment!"

Great. My self-esteem was already so low I could slide under doors. But I stomped out of the room and looked into the nearest mirror. When I came back into the kitchen, I faced him squarely and with conviction I said, "I don't see the woman you see. I see a woman who is slowly but surely taking responsibility for herself. I see a woman who is doing the hard, gut-wrenching work she needs to do to give herself a happy future. I'm sorry you are disappointed, but for the first time in my life I'm beginning to feel like I know who I am. I'm on this path, and your belittling me isn't going to stop me."

With that I picked up the phone to call Mark and wish him a happy birthday. That moment was the turning point for me. I felt like I, too, had just celebrated a birthday. I knew I couldn't be with a man who felt I was nothing but a big disappointment. Things would have to change or I would not stay in this marriage. I started to make plans to move out of the cycle of abuse.

By then I could read Steve like a book. I was able to accurately predict when he was approaching his point of explosion. My therapist was questioning me. "Let's see, Karen, how many cycles of abuse do you want to go through? Three? Four? Ten? Twenty? Let's just figure out how many more times you are willing to let this man beat you up verbally before you call it quits."

~ ~ ~ ~ ~ ~ ~ ~ ~ ~ ~ ~ ~ ~ ~ ~ ~ ~ ~ ~

One day in May, I had a call from a good friend who said, "I just want you to know I gave your name to a recruiter this morning. She is conducting a search for a large retailer in the area for a public relations and communications manager. I told her you would be perfect for the job."

I thanked her and hung up the phone, wondering who it was. Within minutes, the recruiter called me to set up a meeting. Here we go again, I thought. But nothing ventured, nothing gained.

My meeting with the recruiter went well and led to an initial interview with a senior vice president of a large drug store chain. I couldn't believe it. I thoroughly enjoyed my interview and really wanted the job. The company's new CEO was the man to convince, and convince him I did.

I went to my meeting with him — both barrels loaded. I had a list of notes about the company, his job, my job, what his expectations were, and more. As he walked me to the door of his more-than-spacious office (You could have held a bowling tournament in the executive wing of the headquarters building.), he said, "You are one of three candidates. I'll decide by next Friday and let you know."

Confidently, I retorted, "This is my job. You have to let me have it." Driving home on the freeway, I kept replaying that conversation over and over in my head, kicking myself again and again. "You stupid nut. How could you be so obnoxious?" I held my breath for five days, hating myself for wanting that job so badly. But my power play was successful, and I was hired and would start working in ten days. When the recruiter called, she said, "There's white smoke in the chimney."

I was overjoyed. The pay was good. The company was great. Steve was happy to have me bringing home the bacon again. I could still go to school and the company would pay

~ ~ ~ ~ ~ ~ ~ ~ ~ ~ ~ ~ ~ ~ ~ ~ ~ ~ ~ ~

for my classes. They were glad I was getting a degree in communication and gave me the title of director of corporate communication.

I arrived at the headquarters at eight-thirty on June 3, 1991. It felt weird to be getting up early, squeezing into a pair of pantyhose, dressing for success and driving a half-hour down the freeway. I wondered if I was doing the right thing, but I had such high hopes for this job that my concerns flew out the window. I was excited to pull a new corporate communication department together and help the new CEO create a successful company.

I reported to the CEO and worked closely with him. Together we established a credible communication department, and I was promoted to vice president within the year. I was so excited when I was told about my promotion. Little did I know it was one of the worst things that could happen to me.

This company, with 21,000 employees, had less than twenty officers. Officers and staff alike equated a vice president with God. When I was a director I could have lunch with members of the staff in the cafeteria. They would talk to me and I made a few friends; just a few, but it was all right. Once I was promoted to vice president, my friends couldn't relate to me anymore, and the other officers wouldn't talk to me either. I have never felt so isolated among so many people.

It had been my experience that I was accepted for being fun and smart. And most people recognized I had a pretty good heart. Not here. The officers didn't trust me because I reported directly to the CEO, and they didn't want to tell me anything I might carry to him. He ruled pretty much from a fear-based orientation, so people were always nervous and on their toes.

~ ~ ~ ~ ~ ~ ~ ~ ~ ~ ~ ~ ~ ~ ~ ~ ~ ~ ~ ~

I hadn't been there a week when a senior vice president, came raving into my office screaming, "You stay the hell out of my stores!" I was stunned, to say the least, and sat there blinking back tears as he lit into me about something. I tried to calm down and ask him what he was talking about. As it turned out, it wasn't me at all; it was another officer who had apparently violated his stores. He was gone within the month.

Unfortunately, the senior vice president and I never overcame that incident. He scared the hell out of me and he knew it. There was another strike against me. He was a devout Mormon, and he could hear my Utah accent. He was unimpressed upon learning I no longer practiced the Mormon faith.

But the work was wonderful. I hadn't ever been in a situation like that. I enjoyed my staff, and we were successful in building a communication strategy for the company which was consistent, factual and highly effective. We built a television studio so we could communicate with the stores directly using interactive teleconferencing. I spent time lobbying on behalf of the company and meeting with government officials trying to persuade them to see our point of view on a variety of issues important to the continued success of the corporation.

Crisis management became my favorite activity. I loved taking on challenges and developing an intelligent communication strategy to get our point across. It was all new, and I gave it my best shot. But politically, I committed suicide every day without knowing it.

~ ~ ~ ~ ~ ~ ~ ~ ~ ~ ~ ~ ~ ~ ~ ~ ~ ~ ~

I kept taking classes, and finally, miracle of miracles, in December of 1991 I received my bachelor of arts degree in communication. I was going to be a speaker at the ceremony. I was so excited. I had waited a long time for this day. It should have been one of the happiest days of my life. But I woke up so sick that I could hardly lift my head up off the pillow. My dad arrived (we were working on our relationship) to take me to the ceremony and wound up taking me to the hospital. He stayed with me while I spent the day getting IVs then brought me back home and tenderly tucked me back into bed.

Steve had to spill the beans about the surprise party he and Anne had planned. Everybody was coming. I had to get out of bed. And I rose to the occasion. We had a wonderful party with toasts and roasts. It was one of Steve's finest moments.

And I, well, I did finally get what I went after. I had my degree.

※

June, 1992

Dear Mrs. Jackson,

If I thought Wall Street played hardball, I don't have words to describe where I am now. This company is run by little boys trying to be men. I've never seen such an emotional bunch in my life. They don't cry or anything like that. But they sure scream and make fun of each other a lot. No one feels safe around here. Fear rules relentlessly with an iron fist. The CEO is mercurial — friendly one minute, remote and impersonal the next. I'm sure I'll figure him out pretty soon. At least, I hope so.

The senior officers run around in a pack like cub scouts preparing for a hike. They don't allow others into their private circle. I really can't figure

~ ~ ~ ~ ~ ~ ~ ~ ~ ~ ~ ~ ~ ~ ~ ~ ~ ~ ~

out how such a big company can be managed by such small men.

I'm trying hard to make my job work, but it doesn't feel good. I did get promoted, so my work can't be all bad. But if it isn't bad, why does it feel so bad?

Between my job, Steve and my dad, I am tired of trying to understand everyone and myself. Steve and I are still at it. Life's great one week and wretched the next. What do you think I should do? I feel like the person God wanted me to be is about an inch tall.

Oh, by the way, Dad seems to be softening a bit. He sent me a set of tapes by a guy named Deepak Chopra and recommended I listen. This Chopra has a different way of looking at himself in the world. I'm really interested in exploring the spiritual side of my life. I know I can. I am excited. There is a whole new dimension waiting for me to explore, a new door is open for me. This is the path that holds the answers for me — for everybody. It's exciting.

Hope you are well. I miss seeing you. Thanks for staying in touch.

Love,
Karen

The next year fairly flew by. Nothing changed at home or at work. But things did start to move with Dad. He came to Portland and we had a guarded conversation, but a conversation nonetheless. He had become quite enamored with Chopra and wanted to share his message with his children. Anne, my sister Patti and I took to our spiritual

~ ~ ~ ~ ~ ~ ~ ~ ~ ~ ~ ~ ~ ~ ~ ~ ~ ~ ~

awakening as a bird takes to the air. My search was over. Here was a message I could understand. I felt like Deepak Chopra was talking directly to me, and talking about things I knew were real — such as a "field of infinite possibilities" and "the space between the gaps."

I started to focus on myself rather than on everybody else. What a shift in consciousness. Suddenly I was examining myself, and what I was doing to cause the same challenges in my life over and over — and always with men who were important in my life. Like my favorite poet, Edna St. Vincent Millay, said, "Life isn't one damn thing after another. It's the same damn thing over and over."

I slowly became aware that I had created every single event in my life. That was a hard fact to face. There was no one to blame, no one to lay my misery on. On the other hand, it was an incredible feeling to know that I could consciously create my life just as I want it from now on.

My life is in my hands. Nobody has taken advantage of me or abused me without my permission. During the last months of my marriage to Steve and the debacle at the drug store chain I kept posted on my bathroom mirror: "I deserve what I tolerate."

My security and my future are a result of my own choices. I am free to make mistakes and correct them, I am free to express myself any way I choose — from creating a pungent green bean soufflé to planting my back fence with akebia and virginia creeper. My workshops for women about money are my ultimate self-expression. I have identified my life purpose, and I live it day after day.

I was just beginning to come alive.

~ ~ ~ ~ ~ ~ ~ ~ ~ ~ ~ ~ ~ ~ ~ ~ ~ ~ ~ ~

Steve was a stickler for being on time. I would always ask him for the exact time he wanted to leave the house and then made damn sure I was ready on the dot — or there would be hell to pay!

I remember the time I was four minutes late picking up Lisa and Tony to go to parade. Steve was livid. He thought it was setting a terrible example for Tony, who tended to be less than punctual. Steve ignored me all evening, and as soon as we dropped the young people at their apartment, he started yelling at me. The short ride to our apartment was horrible. Steve brought up every thing I had done wrong in my life. He continued his angry tirade even after we arrived home, until he was in such a fit of rage that I crawled under the glass top of the dining room table just to escape his wrath.

It was the end for me when I yelled back, "Leave me alone. Don't you ever do this to me again." I meant it. The next day I packed a bag of clothes and put the bag in the trunk of my car. I told Steve if he ever yelled at me like that again, I would leave.

The verbal attacks I received were as damaging as physical beatings might have been. Some weekends I was literally ill. It was a shocking experience to actually feel physical pain from verbal abuse. Steve could not hurt me more had he taken a two-by-four and whacked me across my back. I literally was in so much pain I couldn't move.

I believed his playing around with the truth was another form of abuse. I no longer believed anything he told me. And lots of times he was telling the truth. It had become impossible to maintain an intimate relationship because of my fear and total distrust of the man I had once loved so passionately. I still loved him, but I couldn't make it work anymore. The year I spent at home set me on a pathway of

~ ~ ~ ~ ~ ~ ~ ~ ~ ~ ~ ~ ~ ~ ~ ~ ~ ~ ~

self-knowledge and self-reliance that made it virtually impossible for me to live in my marriage. Yet I knew Steve loved me deeply in his own way.

I knew it was just a matter of time before we would have to call it quits, and I was more than heartbroken. He was my Prince Charming — yet I finally said goodbye.

My life turned from also-ran to spectacular in August of 1993. Steve had been gone for eight months; he had filed for divorce, and the judgment was sitting on the judge's desk to be signed. I was sad, but absolutely certain I was doing the right thing. On top of that, I sold my big house, bought my little house and — wonder of wonders — I got fired. What a week.

I knew I had to sell my house because it was expensive, and even though I could manage the payments on my salary, I couldn't take care of it without help. I sadly put my dream house on the market.

Looking for a new house was not easy. I had certain ideas of what I wanted. I knew I had to downsize, but I wasn't too keen on the houses in my price range. I remember walking into one cute little house, turning to the realtor with a grimace and saying, "How can I live in such a dinky little house?"

She laughed and said, "There are worse things, Karen."

So, I said, "Okay, I'll take it."

I couldn't have done better if I'd tried. With my favorite pieces of furniture, some good art and a few of my wonderful treasures in place, that dinky little house went overboard to please me. I grew to love it.

~ ~ ~ ~ ~ ~ ~ ~ ~ ~ ~ ~ ~ ~ ~ ~ ~ ~ ~ ~

It was no surprise to me that I was fired. I realized six weeks before that it wasn't a question of "if," it was only a question of "when." After the parent company put the drug store chain on the block, things happened rather swiftly. The CEO promoted his daughter, who worked for me, to the director level and doubled her salary. Not being born yesterday, I knew my department couldn't support both of our salaries, and one of us was going to go. I called a lawyer who specializes in such matters and questioned him about how I should handle my eventual termination. He gave me interesting advice: "Don't have the meeting until you are ready." I took him at his word and took the opportunity to travel throughout the chain, spending as little time in the main office as possible. This gave me a chance for my eventual unemployment to settle in. I had never been fired, and I had never been involuntarily unemployed. It hurt.

Finally, the big day came. The senior vice president's secretary told me he wanted to meet with me at 1:30 that afternoon. When I told her I had a meeting scheduled with the local newspaper, she said, "Cancel it." I knew this was it, yet I felt surprisingly calm. Over lunch with a good friend, I told him, "I need to be back by 1:30 because I'm getting fired today and I don't want to be late."

He said, "You're joking!"

I said, "No, I'll call you about three o'clock this afternoon, probably in tears. The worst part is they will take my car."

And sure enough, by three o'clock that afternoon, the deed was done. I was whisked out of headquarters by a security guard like a prisoner going to an execution. I was driven home and unceremoniously dumped out in my

~ ~ ~ ~ ~ ~ ~ ~ ~ ~ ~ ~ ~ ~ ~ ~ ~ ~ ~

driveway. I choked back the tears as the guard drove off in my car. I recovered enough to call Mark with the good news and bad news. "Hi, Honey. The bad news is I just lost my job. The good news is I have time to move."

When all was said and done, it was the best thing that ever happened to me. To this day I am grateful to that company for teaching me a most useful life lesson.

I am finally free to express myself in my own way, speak in my own voice, and follow my own path.

LIFE LESSONS

ONE WOMAN

My experience with the drug store chain was difficult beyond belief. I felt like I didn't know anything anymore. I just couldn't figure out why people were so mean to me. At least it felt mean. But the worst part was, I treated my staff the same way I was treated. Fear produces fear and we were all afraid. I regret that.

A few months before I was fired, the senior vice president told me angrily, "You know, Karen, you're not as well liked as you think you are." My entire body froze. I couldn't believe my ears. I felt so threatened I didn't sleep night after night.

His accusation rolled over and over in my brain and roared into life to hurt me over and over. Who didn't like me? Why? What could I do about it? Two years later — long after I had put that job behind me — I became acutely aware that if anybody criticized me in the most minor way, I didn't hear what they said, I heard the senior vice president saying, "You know, Karen, you're not as well liked as you think you are."

~ ~ ~ ~ ~ ~ ~ ~ ~ ~ ~ ~ ~ ~ ~ ~ ~ ~ ~ ~

This self-understanding has been a blessing. Coincidentally the day I realized what I was doing, that same senior vice president left me a voice mail. I didn't return the call, but I told my manicurist about it that evening. I shared with her the shame I had felt at his remark, the confusion, the hurt. I turned to her and said, "I wonder what he wanted." Cindy didn't miss a beat and didn't take her eyes off her work, as she said casually, "He probably called to tell you that you're not as well liked as you think you are."

We both laughed out loud, and in that instant, the pain of that traumatic episode dissolved into thin air. Forever. It's only what we give importance to that can overpower us.

Think about your life experiences.
- Where have you felt shame?
- What was it about?
- Was it justified?
- Do you still feel shame about it?
- Do you replay this experience again and again?
- Why?
- Share the experience with someone. It is the only way to heal.

ONE LIFE

Here I was at fifty-two, on my own, truly, for the first time. I felt so grateful to the Universe for giving me the opportunity to grow and experience myself fully. I had a lovely new home and the world hovered at my feet.

I spent a year healing. I had been studying plants and gardening methods for three years. I put my passion to work and planted a miraculous garden. I spent one entire

~ ~ ~ ~ ~ ~ ~ ~ ~ ~ ~ ~ ~ ~ ~ ~ ~ ~ ~ ~

afternoon just watching a twelve-inch patch of ground —
the richness of the earth, the life in every grain of soil and
the mystery of old changing into new. I was new myself. I
would blossom along with those glorious plants. My garden
is the expression of my spirit in the physical world.

I healed my relationship with my dad. I gave up
blaming others for my misfortunes. I became friends with
my soul. For the first time, I knew who I was, and I was
ready to live my vision. I liked myself.

Pay attention to your feelings; they are your guideposts. Honor them. Let them out of their hiding place.
Examine them. Learn from them.

THE MONEY MYSTIQUE

It was hard to sell my house, but I knew the security
of my financial future depended on it. And, as it turned out,
my instinct to pay attention to my money was right on
target. So many women who are in the process of divorce
want to keep the house. I counsel them to think about it
carefully. The comfort of living in the family home pales in
comparison to the drudgery of a burdensome financial
obligation.

I squirreled away as much of my severance pay as I
could. I went from living on several thousand dollars a
month to $1,500 a month. I knew I would be all right
because I didn't have any debt and I had always put money
away for emergencies. I knew I could live for a few years
without any income if I lived frugally.

I just quit spending money, period. I cut out every
unnecessary expense except my manicures. Without them, I
would have felt poor. I actually enjoyed my self-imposed
austerity program. It was a good opportunity for me to call

~ ~ ~ ~ ~ ~ ~ ~ ~ ~ ~ ~ ~ ~ ~ ~ ~ ~ ~ ~

upon my creativity. When we just throw money at a problem, we shortchange ourselves. It is much more fun to find a creative, low-cost solution.

For example, I drove too near a post in a parking garage one afternoon. I was horrified to drive away with the right door mirror dangling precariously until it flew off as I rounded a corner. The replacement cost at the garage was nearly $500, including parts and labor. I almost collapsed. So I called wrecking yards once a month for three months until I finally found a match. I paid less for the mirror installed than I would have paid for the mirror itself. I felt so smart. And I learned wrecking-yard language as well. In the old days, I would have just gulped and bit the $500 bullet. I was willing to wait until I found the perfect mirror at the perfect price.

In my workshops I discuss various ways to save money and to avoid spending it. The discussion focuses on spending consciously, rather than from habit. There are also excellent books about saving money. My favorite is, *How to Pinch a Penny Till It Screams,* by Rochelle LaMotte McDonald.

Money management begins when you make the choice to open your wallet and pull out your credit card, your cash or your checkbook. Think about it before you do it. It is the unconscious spending decisions, our habits, that keep us from enjoying our money.

I have seen women who spend over $1,000 a year on lattes and scones! I would never suggest that you not spend that kind of money for refreshments and snacks. I only suggest that, if you are, know you are. Make a conscious choice to buy a latte and a scone every day and put it into your spending plan. I have another client who buys pizza for the family every Friday night. They realized they spent

~ ~ ~ ~ ~ ~ ~ ~ ~ ~ ~ ~ ~ ~ ~ ~ ~ ~ ~ ~

$857 on pizza in the past eighteen months. This gives them family time together and is a good use of their life energy. It isn't about the money; it's about enjoying what money can buy. Don't stop spending; start enjoying it more.

It is rewarding to use my money to express myself. When my friends ask me why I can't go out to dinner, I reply, "I'm not expressing myself that way right now. I'm building a business."

Seriously examine how you use your money.
- Do you use it to impress yourself?
- Do you use it to impress others?
- Do you use it to honor yourself?
- Do you use it in alignment with your values?
- Are you using too much of your life energy in the pursuit of money?
- Where is the balance for you?
- Do you enjoy your money?
- What steps can you take to enjoy your money more?
- Read, study, learn about yourself.
- Read, study and learn how the money game is played.
- You are a success already, just by reading this book.

EPILOGUE

~ ~ ~ ~ ~ ~ ~ ~ ~ ~ ~ ~ ~ ~ ~ ~ ~ ~

"Life must be lived forwards but can only be understood backwards."
– Nietzche

As I look back on the past three years, I can only say they have been the most rewarding years of my life. I stopped dancing to somebody else's tune. I play my own music now, and I lead!

My business, The Money Mystique, is in its third year and growing strong. My marketing efforts have paid off, and some days I have more calls than I can handle. My biggest challenge is to find balance. It seems when I get one part of my life in alignment, the other part topples off its foundation.

I have worked two years non-stop getting my message out.

~ ~ ~ ~ ~ ~ ~ ~ ~ ~ ~ ~ ~ ~ ~ ~ ~ ~ ~

Women have to take responsibility for themselves. The days of Prince Charming are over. It's time for women to step up and seize their own power and take care of themselves and their money.

In the course of my work, I speak to female audiences all the time about The Money Mystique. When I first started talking to groups of women, I thought they'd throw tomatoes at me to get me off my soapbox. But things have changed. Even though the message is frank and sometimes disturbing about the adjustments they have to make that are not always easy, women take to it like ducks take to water.

I have met the most wonderful women in the world through my business and social life, all of whom have special gifts and talents. It is rewarding to watch these women grow and experience themselves in new and effective ways.

In 1994, I took a spiritual sabbatical and traveled to Nepal and Tibet. I'm still not sure what I was seeking, but I experienced a different spiritual awakening — a deep knowing that I have the power to express myself any way I choose. It is up to me. Nepal and Tibet exude their own special energy, and I was there — in the midst of it. I experienced my soul, my own spirituality, and listened to my inner voice. I'm not the same person after having climbed the mountain. The journey to the top of the world was physically demanding and spiritually renewing. I am more me than ever before.

The road to self-discovery takes time, energy and constant reflection. As Plato said, "The life which is not examined is not worth living." I've learned not to take myself too seriously. I reframe most of my daily events from a negative interpretation to a positive one. Sometimes, I must admit, it takes a few days to understand and rejoice

~ ~ ~ ~ ~ ~ ~ ~ ~ ~ ~ ~ ~ ~ ~ ~ ~ ~ ~

in the lesson.

Universal principles demonstrate that everything in the Universe is perfect, including us. There are no mistakes or failures. It is only our ego that compels us to judge ourselves and each other by uncharitable standards.

God is in us and we are in God. The two cannot be separated. We live in fear when we separate ourselves from the source of all creation. When we are at one with the Universe, we live in freedom and love. Some days I am overwhelmed by the beauty of the earth and the willingness of people to put themselves on the line every single day. It's true: there are no guarantees, and I don't want any.

A friend once introduced me as, "Here's a woman who is way out over her skis." I laughed at the time, but I feel complimented today. Change doesn't happen in the middle. It only happens when we venture over to the edge and take one small step after another. André Gide said it best: "One does not discover new lands without consenting to lose sight of the shore for a very long time." You'd best be the master of your own ship rather than drift along behind someone else's. Speak in your own voice.

Dear Karen,

Surprise! A letter from me and it's not even your birthday? But I needed to gather my thoughts and the telephone just wouldn't work. I left your newest home yesterday — and while I helped you move into an empty house, I am struck by how you have made it uniquely yours.

As long as I have known you, from the first "starter" house, to this wonderful new home, you have always chosen to surround yourself with

~ ~ ~ ~ ~ ~ ~ ~ ~ ~ ~ ~ ~ ~ ~ ~ ~ ~ ~ ~

beautiful things. You have the talent to create harmonious surrounding using imagination and good taste.

Every corner of your new home reflects your sense of beauty and unique style. I see treasures you have had for years, all meaningful and well cared for. Often you find new and unusual settings for some of your pieces — a chaise lounge in the kitchen? You have always told me to "buy the best and take good care of it." Well, you certainly practice what you preach.

Your crowning achievement is your glorious garden. As usual, you immersed yourself in researching and planning the garden long before you ever began. You prepared the soil like you were going to plant gold or something. But you have created a wonderland — from the whimsy of a mirror propped against a fence leading to a fantasy garden beyond to a ceramic bunny hiding among the big leaves of a tall plant. But, Karen, the most important thing as that you have created a haven for your pleasure and comfort — not to make a fashion statement.

I have learned much from you. One of the most important lessons is how to think "taxi — not bus," and to choose spending money on beauty to enrich our lives. For that I am grateful and I love you.

Gloria.

~ ~ ~ ~ ~ ~ ~ ~ ~ ~ ~ ~ ~ ~ ~ ~ ~ ~ ~

LIFE LESSONS

ONE LIFE

My life today is calm. I couldn't ask for anything more. I live without conflict, either internal or external. I am pursuing my life work. I enjoy having my own business, and I am successful beyond my wildest dreams. It is a blessing to create money in my life by helping women create and use money in their lives. Word of mouth is powerful, and the women just keep coming. I have seen hundreds of women change their relationship with money and learn to live in harmony with themselves and their money. It isn't really about money, anyway. It's about self-expression and living authentically. We all want to be treasured for who we really are.

As I look over my life and the people who have influenced me, I feel indebted to each one for his or her special contribution. I have learned from every one of them, and each person has changed me in some way. Sometimes I am overwhelmed with gratitude for the challenges I have faced. Each one has led me inward to my essence. Each one has forged a stronger steel rod up my back. And each one has enriched me in ways I can barely fathom.

Steve has already moved on to a new life and family, and I only wish for him the very best. He was a great teacher. He taught me how to use my calculator. He taught me to speak in public without being afraid. He introduced me to chess and tennis. He helped me be strong enough to stand up for myself.

Lisa is wonderful. She and her new mate plan to marry soon. She has a great job with a bank and was recently offered a handsome promotion. She loves graduate school.

~ ~ ~ ~ ~ ~ ~ ~ ~ ~ ~ ~ ~ ~ ~ ~ ~ ~ ~

Words can't express my respect, love and admiration for her spirit and determination to choose health and life.

Last year Mark moved to Atlanta. He stays in touch by phone and is a man I am proud to know, let alone call my son. Both kids follow the guidelines of the Money Mystique and live in harmony with money.

Anne is still there beside me all the way. What a gift it has been to have a sister in the same city to share life's passages. I thank God for my entire family, which is grounded in love, laughter and support.

Dad is eighty years old now and dancing the years away. He always was a fun dancer. He led us to our spiritual awakening. This is his greatest legacy. Thank you, Dad, for showing us the way.

Steadfast Gary is the most loving father in the world. He has loved and supported Lisa and Mark in ways many fathers don't even dream about. I am happy to have shared my children with him.

I am grateful to all my friends for laughing at my stories and believing in me.

Finally, a big thanks to all the men who hired me; I appreciate your confidence.

Life wasn't always easy, but for the most part it was fun.

THE MONEY MYSTIQUE

Think about The Money Mystique and how it applies to you. Do you take responsibility for yourself, or do you believe someone else should have that obligation? It isn't about money; it's about you and self-esteem and free will and self-expression.

It has taken me a lifetime to get over the feeling that

~ ~ ~ ~ ~ ~ ~ ~ ~ ~ ~ ~ ~ ~ ~ ~ ~ ~ ~

somebody else should support me. I think it's in my DNA. Believe me, even if it is biological, it doesn't work anymore. Maybe we women cooked our own goose when we marched on Washington and clamored for equality.

I don't know about you, but I wouldn't have it any other way. Once you get used to your independence, once you understand your power and are in control of your body, your time, and your money, you can relax and enjoy the abundance the Universe has to offer.

I have abundance unbounded in my own life. As I look at my garden, I see the flowers tumbling over each other in their attempt to be seen. I see the mirror in the garden reflect the cool, green ground covers. My life overflows with an abundance of friends, clients and family who support me in all ways. We laugh together and we cry together.

There is a natural order to the Universe that supports us totally, so we can relax and enjoy the abundance that is our birthright.

Namasté

~ ~ ~ ~ ~ ~ ~ ~ ~ ~ ~ ~ ~ ~ ~ ~ ~ ~ ~ ~

75 Ways To Conquer the Money Mystique

~ ~ ~ ~ ~ ~ ~ ~ ~ ~ ~ ~ ~ ~ ~ ~ ~ ~

1. Take responsibility for yourself.
2. Tell the truth.
3. Forgive yourself and others every day.
4. Simplify your life.
5. Downsize.
6. Take care of your body.
7. Love and nurture your partner.
8. Love and nurture your children.
9. Love and nurture your friendships.
10. Love and nurture yourself.
11. Reduce, reuse, recycle.
12. Take care of the planet.
13. Volunteer.
14. Buy the best you can afford and take care of it.
15. Make peace with your mother.
16. Make peace with your father.

~ ~ ~ ~ ~ ~ ~ ~ ~ ~ ~ ~ ~ ~ ~ ~ ~ ~ ~ ~

17. When you feel afraid, tell yourself, *"I have every-thing I need right now."*
18. Plant a garden.
19. Spend time alone.
20. Turn off your television.
21. Read a good book.
22. Talk nicely to yourself.
23. Find time each day to play.
24. Get a cat.
25. Use your money consciously.
26. Buy fresh flowers once a week.
27. Love your body, be sexual.
28. Enjoy your money.
29. Live beneath your means.
30. Invest in stocks.
31. Get enough sleep.
32. Figure out what you don't want in your life.
33. Make friends with men.
34. Make friends with older women.
35. Make friends with younger women.
36. Talk to your daughters about being a woman.
37. Tell your partner what makes your heart sing.
38. Enjoy silence.
40. Only stay in relationships that support you.
41. Keep your promises.
42. Thank the Universe every day for giving you life's challenges.
43. Believe you deserve only good things.
44. Know when you have your heart's desire.
45. Accept what you cannot change.
46. Don't worry.
47. Be patient.
48. Join a support group.

~ ~ ~ ~ ~ ~ ~ ~ ~ ~ ~ ~ ~ ~ ~ ~ ~ ~ ~ ~

49. Keep a journal.
50. Draw pictures of your life as you envision it.
51. Wear sexy underwear, even if you live alone.
52. Be patient and give up attachment to the outcome.
53. Feel your feelings.
54. Go to church.
55. Trust in the wisdom of the Universe.
56. Take a bath in candlelight.
57. Live your life purpose.
58. Go see the other side of the world.
59. Balance your checkbook every month.
60. Meditate every day.
61. Pay your bills on time.
62. Have a psychic reading.
63. Be happy with what you have.
64. Rejoice in the success of others.
65. Remember your friend's birthdays.
66. Talk about your childhood with your brothers and sisters.
67. Know you have the power to create your life just as you want it.
68. Believe in yourself.
69. Write down your sleeping dreams.
70. Learn to use a computer.
71. Visualize yourself having everything you desire.
72. Write your own story.
73. Live without shame.
74. Stop pretending.
75. **Never take no for an answer.**

~ ~ ~ ~ ~ ~ ~ ~ ~ ~ ~ ~ ~ ~ ~ ~ ~ ~ ~ ~

BIBLIOGRAPHY

~ ~ ~ ~ ~ ~ ~ ~ ~ ~ ~ ~ ~ ~ ~ ~ ~ ~ ~

Barron's (editor), *Dictionary of Finance and Investment Terms,* Barron's Business guides.

Bogle, John C., *Bogle on Mutual Funds,* Irwin Publishing, 1994.

Briles, Judith, *Money Sense, What Every Woman Must Know to be Financially Confident,* Moody Press, 1995.

Cameron, Julia, *The Artist's Way,* Tarcher/Putnam, 1992.

Chopra, Deepak, *The Seven Spiritual Laws of Success,* Amber Allen Publishing, 1994.

Dominguez, Joe and Robin, Vicki, *Your Money or Your Life,* Viking, 1992.

Estes, Clarissa Pinkola, *Women Who Run with The Wolves,* Ballantine, 1992.

Gawain, Shakti, *Creative Visualization,* Bantam Books, 1978.

Heilbroner, Robert and Thurow, Lester, *Economics Explained,* Touchstone, 1994.

Leeds, Dorothy, *Smart Questions to Ask Your Stockbroker,* Harper, 1993.

Leonard, Frances, *Money and the Mature Woman,* Addison

~ ~ ~ ~ ~ ~ ~ ~ ~ ~ ~ ~ ~ ~ ~ ~ ~ ~ ~ ~

Wesley, 1993.

McDonald, Rochell LaMotte, *How to Pinch a Penny Till It Screams,* Avery Publishing Group, 1994.

Mellon, Olivia, *Money Harmony ... Resolving Money Conflicts in Your Life and Relationships,* Walker and Company, 1994.

Miller, Theodore J., *Invest Your Way to Wealth,* Kiplinger's Books, 1994

Morris, Kenneth M. and Siegel, alan M., *The Wall Street Guide To Understanding Personal Finance,* Fireside Press, 1992.

Roman, Sanaya and Packer, Duane, *Creating Money,* HJ Kramer Inc., 1988.

Ross, Ruth, *Prospering Woman,* New World Library, 1982.

Sharamon, Shalila and Baginski, Bodo J., *The Chakra Handbook,* Lotus Light Publications, 1991.

Siegel, Jeremy J., *Stocks for the Long Run,* Irwin, 1994.

Sinetar, Marsha, *Do What You Love, The Money Will Follow,* Dell, 1987.

St. James, Elaine, *Inner Simplicity,* Hyperion, 1994.

St. James, Elaine, *Simplify Your Life,* Hyperion, 1994.

White, Shelby, *What Every Woman Should Know About Her Husband's Money,* Turtle Bay Books, 1992.

To order additional copies of

NEVER TAKE NO FOR AN ANSWER

Book: $14.95   Shipping/Handling $3.50

BookPartners, Inc.
Phone: 1-800-895-7323
Fax: 503-682-8684

To contact Karen Sheridan for personal coaching,
seminars, speaking appearances, newsletter or
other educational products

Phone: 503-620-5098
or
e-mail: Makewealth @ AOL.COM